W9-CVZ-241

Effective Outlines
and Illustrations

Effective Outlines and Illustrations

By
HYMAN J. APPELMAN

BAKER BOOK HOUSE
Grand Rapids, Michigan

ISBN: 0-8010-0043-2

Reprinted 1972 by
Baker Book House Company

Copyright, 1949, by
Hyman J. Appelman

PHOTOLITHOPRINTED BY CUSHING - MALLOY, INC.
ANN ARBOR, MICHIGAN, UNITED STATES OF AMERICA
1972

Review Copy

Your courtesy in announcing and reviewing this book in your periodical will be appreciated. It will be an added kindness if you will send a marked copy of your review issue to

BAKER BOOK HOUSE, *Grand Rapids, Michigan 49506*

Editors will be pleased to know that in most instances portions or chapters of this publication may be reprinted in their periodical without cost. However, written permission is necessary, which may be obtained by writing to the Editorial Department of Baker Book House. Thank you!

CONTENTS

Study to shew thyself approved unto God, a workman that needeth not to be ashamed, rightly dividing the word of truth.
—II Timothy 2:15

OUTLINES

1

GOD THE LIGHT-GIVER
Genesis 1:3

I. LIGHT IS ACCORDING TO GOD'S WILL
   A. God is.
   B. God wills.
   C. God acts.
II. LIGHT COMES AT THE WORD OF GOD
   A. By His power.
   B. Suddenly (Heb. 11:3).
III. GOD'S LIGHT MEETS THE NEEDS OF MAN
   A. Essential to man's bodily comfort.
   B. Adequate to man's mental development.
   C. Meets the needs of the soul (Heb. 12:3).

❋   ❋   ❋

2

HIDING FROM GOD
Genesis 3:8-10

I. WHY MEN HIDE
   A. Fear caused by God's holiness (Exod. 3:6; Isa. 6;
      Rev. 1:17).
   B. Fear caused by man's sinfulness.
II. WHERE MEN HIDE
   A. Behind false hopes.

B. Behind indifference.
C. Behind excuses.
D. Behind self-righteous acts.
E. Behind innocence.
F. Behind ignorance.

III. THE IMPOSSIBILITY OF HIDING

A. Prov. 28:13.
B. Amos 9:2-4.
C. Ps. 139:7-12.
D. Jonah 1:3.

IV. ONLY ONE SAFE HIDING PLACE: Jesus (Rev. 6:12-17)

❈   ❈   ❈

3

CHRIST'S WORK—ATONEMENT
Leviticus 15

I. RECONCILIATION

A. The fruit of the atonement (II Cor. 5:18-20).
B. God glorified by the shed and sprinkled blood, bearing away the sins of the people (atonement).

II. SUBSTITUTION

A. Transference of the sins of the people to head of scapegoat, and its dismissal to a land not inhabited.
B. A believer's truth, not universal (I Cor. 15:3; I Pet. 2:24; Isa. 53:6; Heb. 10:17).

III. PROPITIATION

A. The blessed work done within the veil and before the eye of God.
B. The blessed answer of Jesus meeting in death and

before God the holy and righteous claim of Jehovah's throne.

C. Christ now God's propitiation or mercy seat (Rom. 3:25; I John 1:7; Heb. 2:17).

❊   ❊   ❊

4

THE SCARLET THREAD IN THE OLD TESTAMENT
Leviticus 17:11; Genesis 22:6-8; Isaiah 53:4-6; Zechariah 13:1

I. THE PROVISION OF THE BLOOD

A. God's plan—revealed from above, not evolved from below.

B. Binding upon *all* Jews alike.

C. Foreshadowing Christ—Paul's schoolmaster.

II. THE PROPERTIES OF THE BLOOD

A. Redeems—as Passover lamb, as offering for firstborn, thus averting the wrath of God (Isa. 53:4-6).

B. Covers (Lev. 17:11; Isa. 44:25; 45:22).

C. Cleanses (Zech. 13:1).

D. Consecrates.

III. THE PREACHING OF THE BLOOD

A. Our only message for a lost world.

B. Contra every other scheme and plan.

C For salvation (Isa. 55:1).

D. For separation (Rom. 12:1-2; I Cor. 6:19-20).

E. For service (Hab. 12:1-2; Phil. 2:5-8).

❊   ❊   ❊

5

THE CHRISTIAN LIFE
Deuteronomy 6

I. A RICH LIFE (vs. 3)
II. A GIFTED LIFE (vs. 10)
III. A HOLY LIFE (vs. 13)
IV. A CONQUERING LIFE (vs. 19)
V. AN ESTABLISHED LIFE (vs. 23)
VI. A SURE LIFE (vs. 25)

❃   ❃   ❃

6

THE CROSSING OF JORDAN
Joshua 3

I. PREPARATION FOR JORDAN
   A. By instruction.
      1. To Joshua—from heaven (Josh. 3:7-8).
      2. To people—from Joshua (Josh. 3:12-13; 3:3-4).
   B. By sanctification (Josh. 3:5).
      1. Like Samson who was separated unto God (Judg. 13:5).
      2. Like the first-born of Israel (Exod. 13:2).
   C. By exhortation.
      1. To be ready to follow (Josh. 3:3-4).
      2. To be assured of safety (Josh. 3:5).

II. THE PARTING OF JORDAN
   A. God's power vindicated (Josh. 3:10).
   B. God's potentate honored (Josh. 4:14).
   C. God's promise fulfilled (Josh. 3:7).

III. The Passage through Jordan
   A. Was by faith (Josh. 3:13).
   B. Was in order (Josh. 3:14-17).
   C. Was for victory (Josh. 1:11).
                          —E. A. Entner

❀   ❀   ❀

7

CALEB—THE MAN FOR THE TIMES
Joshua 14:8

I. Caleb's Faithful Following of His God
   A. Universally without dividing.
   B. Fully and sincerely without dissembling.
   C. Wholly and cheerfully without disputing.
   D. Constantly without declining.

II. Caleb's Favored Portion
   A. His life preserved in the hour of judgment.
   B. Comforted with a long life of vigor.
   C. Received great honor among his brethren.
   D. Distinguished by being put upon the hardest service.
   E. Enjoyed what he had once seen.
   F. Left a blessing for his children.

III. Caleb's Secret, Forceful Character
   A. Bold.
   B. Generous.
   C. Courageous.
   D. Noble heroic spirit.

IV. The Spirit Needed by Today's Calebs
   A. A spirit of faith.
   B. A meek spirit.
   C. A brave spirit.

D. A loving spirit.
E. A zealous spirit.
F. A heavenly spirit.

❅   ❅   ❅

8

THE WORTHIEST RESOLUTION
Joshua 24:15

I. PERSONAL
II. PARENTAL
III. PRACTICAL
IV. PROFESSED
V. PERMANENT

❅   ❅   ❅

9

SAMSON A TYPE OF THE CHRISTIAN
Judges 14:5-7

I. HUMAN VACUITY—EMPTINESS
   A. The strain of life.
   B. The sorrows of life.
II. HEAVENLY VITALITY—ENERGY
   A. Common.
   B. Conditional.
   C. Constraining—costly.
III. HAPPY VICTORY—EFFECTIVENESS
   A. Self.
   B. Circumstances.
   C. Souls.

—Vance Havner

❅   ❅   ❅

10

DIVINE DELIVERANCE
I Samuel 7:1-6

I. Through the Agency of a Personal Deliverer
II. Upon the Conditions of Sincere Repentance for Sin and a Wholehearted Return to the Lord
III. Through a Covenant Sealed with Blood
IV. In Answer to Prayer
V. Through the Use of Appointed Means

✳   ✳   ✳

11

A WISE YOUNG MAN
II Samuel 18:29; Ecclesiastes 11:9; 12:1

I. His Life—How Will He Use it?
  A. A wrong use: Luke 12:16-21.
  B. A right use: Rom. 14:7-9; Phil. 1:21.
II. His Walk—Which Way Will He Go?
  A. The wrong way: Ps. 36:4; Prov. 13:15; 14:12; 12:15-26; 7:8-27.
  B. The right way: Prov. 3:17; 4:18; 6:6; John 14:6; Hos. 10:20.
III. His Judgment—How Will He Stand? (John 5:24; Ps. 1:4-6; John 3:18, 36)
IV. His Safeguard—How Secured? (Eccles. 12; Isa. 55: 6-11)

✳   ✳   ✳

12

THE ANNALS OF A CONTINUOUS REVIVAL AND POWER
II Kings 2

   I. PRAYER (vss. 9, 14)
  II. THE WATERS OF JERICHO HEALED (vs. 21)
 III. BETHEL'S INSOLENCE REBUKED (vs. 23)
  IV. VALLEY FILLED WITH WATER (3:20)
   V. WIDOW'S OIL MULTIPLIED (4:6)
  VI. SHUNAMMITE'S SON RESTORED (4:36)
 VII. POTTAGE SWEETENED (4:41)
VIII. NAAMAN'S LEPROSY CURED (5:14)
  IX. AXE AFLOAT (6:6)
   X. GOD'S CHARIOTS AT DOTHAN (6:17)
  XI. SAMARIA DELIVERED (7:16)
 XII. PARALLELS IN CHRISTIAN EXPERIENCE (vss. 6, 7)
       A. Past testimonies.
       B. Present testings.
       C. Power triumphing.
       D. We face.
       E. We have.
       F. We need.

❋   ❋   ❋

13

CONSECRATION
I Chronicles 29:5

  I. A CALL (I Chron. 29:5)
 II. A DUTY (Ex. 32:29; Num. 6:12; Rev. 1:6; Ezek. 43:26;
     II Cor. 6:17; Acts 24:16; Rom. 13:14; 12:1; Eph. 6:11;
     II Cor. 5:15; I Cor. 6:19-20)
III. A FIRST DUTY (I Chron. 29:5; Matt. 6:33; I Tim. 4:8;
     I Kings 3:5-13; Mark 10:29-30)

IV. Must Be Willing (I Chron. 29:5; Gen. 35; Ps. 110:3; Judg. 5:2; I Chron. 29:9; I Pet. 5:2)
V. Must Be Entire (Matt. 6:24; Rom. 13:14; I Cor. 10:31; Col. 3:17; II Tim. 2:19-22)

❋   ❋   ❋

14

SIGNS OF A REVIVAL
Ezra 9:8

I. A Fresh Quickening of God's People
II. A Revived Spirit of Prayer
III. An Increased Love of Precious Souls
IV. Efforts Made Answering to This Love
V. An Enlarged Expectation of Blessing

❋   ❋   ❋

15

NEHEMIAH'S PRAYER
Nehemiah 1

I. Reveals Earnestness
II. Reveals Adoration
III. Contains the Elements of Confession
IV. Evidences Unselfishness
V. Pleading on Basis of Promises and Former Blessings
VI. Exercises Faith
VII. Is Definite
VIII. Reveals Perseverance

❋   ❋   ❋

16

OUR SINS
Job 13

I. THEY STICK
II. THEY COME BACK AS BITTER MEMORIES
III. THEY ARE DISQUALIFYING INFIRMITIES
IV. THEY ARE GUILTY BURDENS
V. THEY ARE MOTIVES TO SEEK GOD'S MERCY

❀   ❀   ❀

17

THE GODLY AND THE UNGODLY
Psalm 1

I. THE UNGODLY
    A. Without God.
    B. Estranged from God.
    C. Against God.
    D. "Standeth in the way of sinners."
       1. Approves their conduct.
       2. Applauds their evil.
       3. Enters into their iniquities.
    E. "Sitteth in the seat of the scornful."
       1. Critics.
       2. Gossips.
       3. Jealous-hearted.
II. THE GODLY
    A. "Delight."
       1. To know.
       2. To do.
       3. To teach.

B. "Meditate."
   1. Study.
   2. Search.
   3. Apply.
C. Are "like a tree."
   1. Strong.
   2. Unshakeable.
   3. Helpful.
   4. Fruitful.

❋   ❋   ❋

18

REDEMPTION
Psalm 49

I. ITS SUBJECT—THE SOUL
II. ITS POWERS—KNOWLEDGE AND CHOICE
III. ITS AFFECTIONS—GOD OR SIN
IV. ITS DURATION—FOREVER
V. ITS PRICE—VAST; PRECIOUS

❋   ❋   ❋

19

CHRIST THE GREAT EMANCIPATOR
Psalm 146:7

I. DELIVERS FROM THE PENALTY OF SIN BY HIS ATONING DEATH (I Pet. 2:24)
II. DELIVERS FROM THE POWER OF SIN BY HIS RISEN POWER (Col. 2:12-13)
III. DELIVERS FROM THE POLLUTION OF SIN BY HIS INDWELLING PRESENCE (John 15:4-5)

IV. DELIVERS FROM THE PAUPERISM OF SIN BY THE RICHES OF HIS GRACE (Eph. 2:7)
V. DELIVERS FROM THE PLEASURE OF SIN BY THE PLEASURE IN HIS RIGHT HAND (Ps. 16:11, R.V.)
VI. DELIVERS FROM THE PRINCIPLE OF SIN BY HIS OPERATING LOVE (I John 3:6)
VII. DELIVERS FROM THE PRESENCE OF SIN AT HIS GLORIOUS RETURN (Phil. 3:20-21)

❋   ❋   ❋

20

GOD'S COMMAND
Proverbs 23:26

I. THE REALM
   A. Affections of the soul.
   B. Confidence of the mind.
   C. Service of the life (John 14:15, 21; I John 2:3-5; 5:3).
II. THE RULE
III. THE REASONABLENESS OF THIS COMMAND (Rom. 12:1 —"reasonable service")
   A. His right over us as our Creator.
   B. His mercies toward us as our Redeemer.
   C. His relation to us as our Father.
   D. The utter worthlessness of all His competitors.

❋   ❋   ❋

21

THE GIFT OF SALVATION
Isaiah 55:1

I. THE FREENESS OF THE OFFERED GIFT
II. THE UNIVERSALITY OF THE OFFERED GIFT OF SALVATION

A. Offered to all nations of mankind.
B. Offered to men of every state, class and character.
C. Is free to the chief of sinners.
D. Ought, therefore, to be considered by each individual hearer as addressed personally to himself.

�֍   �֍   ✖

22

THREE WONDERFUL THEMES OF OLD TESTAMENT PROPHECY

I. A WONDERFUL PERSON
   A. "The seed of the woman."
   B. "The son of David."
   C. "The Redeemer."
   D. "Israel's Messiah."
   E. "The Lord and king of the whole earth."

II. A WONDERFUL PEOPLE (Jer. 31:35-37; Isa. 44:6-7—"My people")
   A. An everlasting nation.
   B. Loved with His everlasting love (Jer. 31:3).
   C. Named with an everlasting name (Isa. 56:5).
   D. Saved according to the terms of the "everlasting covenant." (Jer. 32:40).
   E. To be ruled by an everlasting King (Jer. 10:10).

III. A WONDERFUL POSSESSION (Gen. 15:18)
   1. The promised seed of Genesis.
   2. The Passover Lamb of Exodus.
   3. The perfect sacrifices of Leviticus.
   4. The life-giving serpent of Numbers.
   5. The accessible refuge of Deuteronomy.
   6. The gracious Saviour of Joshua.

7. The mighty man of valor of Judges.
8. The Kinsman-Redeemer of Ruth.
9. The dependent conqueror of Samuel.
10. The glorious King of kings.
11. The vigilant administrator of Chronicles.
12. The wise leader of Ezra.
13. The prayerful builder of Nehemiah.
14. The prevailing intercessor of Esther.
15. The delivering daysman of Job.
16. The patient sufferer of the Psalms.
17. The upright son of Proverbs.
18. The wise man of Ecclesiastes.
19. The attractive beloved of Canticles.
20. The beautiful messenger of Isaiah.
21. The weeping prophet of Jeremiah.
22. The glorious one of Ezekiel.
23. The cut-off Prince of Daniel.
24. The refreshing dew of Hosea.
25. The resolute judge of Joel.
26. The raiser-up of Amos.
27. The satisfying possession of Obadiah.
28. The afflicted substitute of Jonah.
29. The caster-away of sins of Micah.
30. The irresistible stronghold of Nahum.
31. The holy searcher of Habakkuk.
32. The glad singer of Zephaniah.
33. The faithful blesser of Haggai.
34. The smitten shepherd of Zechariah.
35. The coming refiner of Malachi.

* * *

23

THE FAITH CONDITION
Isaiah 7:9

I. FAITH IS THE ONE UNIVERSAL CONDITION THAT DEMANDS AND RIGHTEOUSLY DEMANDS
   A. Because of what He is.
   B. Because of what He is in relation to us.
   C. Because of what He has already done for His people, in the experience of which we have shared.

II. GOD REQUIRED FAITH OF THE PATRIARCHS, ENOCH, NOAH, ABRAHAM

III. GOD REQUIRED FAITH OF THE ISRAELITES—FORTY-YEARS-OF-TRUST LESSON (Heb. 3:19)

IV. GOD REQUIRED FAITH OF THE KINGS
   A. Mission of Elijah.
   B. Reigns of Asa, Jehoshaphat, Hezekiah.

V. GOD REQUIRED FAITH WHEN SPEAKING THROUGH CHRIST TO MEN
   A. Endeavored to secure faith in sufferers before He healed them.
   B. Reproached His disciples for their lack of faith.

VI. FAITH IS GOD'S NECESSARY CONDITION FOR US

❀   ❀   ❀

24

A GRACIOUS INVITATION
Isaiah 55

I. THE STATE OF THE PERSON ADDRESSED
II. THE NATURE OF THE PROVISION PREPARED
III. THE FORCE OF THE INVITATION OFFERED

IV. THE EXTENT OF THE CALL
V. THE FREENESS OF THE SUPPLY
VI. THE SUFFICIENCY OF THE PROVISION
VII. THE IMPOSSIBILITY OF FINDING REDEMPTION ELSEWHERE

❊   ❊   ❊

25

THE BEST BARGAIN
Isaiah 55:1

I. WITHOUT MONEY (Job 34:19; 36:19)
II. WITHOUT PRICE (Rom. 3:24; Gal. 1:4; Gal. 2:20; I Pet. 1:18-19
III. WITHOUT WORKS (Eph. 2:9; Rom. 4:4-5; II Tim. 1:9; Titus 3:5; Rom. 3:28)
IV. WITHOUT WAITING (II Cor. 6:2; Rom. 16:3; Heb. 3:5)

❊   ❊   ❊

26

THE GREATEST INVITATION
Isaiah 55:1

I. SEEK THE KNOWLEDGE OF THE LORD (John 1:18; Eph. 1:17; I Cor. 4:6; I John 5:20; Matt. 11:27)
II. SEEK HIS FAVOR
III. SEEK HIS IMAGE (Eph. 4:22-24)
IV. SEEK COMMUNION WITH HIM (Eph. 4:18; Col. 1:21; I Cor. 6:16; John 14:25; Eph. 2:21-22; I John 1:3)
V. SEEK THE EVERLASTING VISION AND ENJOYMENT OF HIM (Matt. 5:8; I John 3:2; Rev. 21:3-7; 22:3-4)

❊   ❊   ❊

27

BROKEN CISTERNS
Jeremiah 2:13

I. SENSUALISM
The pampered appetite becomes the jaded appetite, and at length becomes the diseased and ruined appetite.

II. WEALTH
The feeder of avarice, not its satisfaction.

III. INTELLECTUALISM
Shows limitations of men's wisdom.
Impossible to grasp mysteries of God, even of life.

IV. MORALITY
Are there any leaks here?
Is cistern perfect?

❋   ❋   ❋

28

BROKEN CISTERNS
Jeremiah 2:13

I. ALL MEN NEED SPIRITUAL REFRESHMENT
A. The soul has its thirst (Ps. 63:1).
B. Spiritual thirst is intensified by the experiences of life.

II. THEY WHO FORSAKE GOD INJURE THEIR OWN SOULS
A. Now, in this life, they experience the loss of God.
B. His refreshing grace is ever flowing, in great abundance, not limited in quantity, and it may be had at all times.
1. It is fresh, like a mountain stream, bubbling

forth cool (water) from the rock; it is not like the stale waters of a cistern.

2. It is wholesome and invigorating, not like the earthy waters of a cistern.

III. THE INJURY ARISING FROM FORSAKING GOD IS INTENSIFIED BY THE UNSATISFACTORY NATURE OF THE SUBSTITUTES TO WHICH MEN TURN
   A. They are self-made.
   B. They are limited in supply.
   C. They are often impure.
   D. They are imperfect even of their kind.

❊   ❊   ❊

29

THE STAIN OF SIN
Jeremiah 2:22

I. SIN STAINS THE CHARACTER AND THE LIFE OF MAN
   A. Leaves stains behind it—internal and external.
   B. These stains are not natural.
   C. They are all evil things.

II. NO MAN CAN WASH THE GUILT OF SIN FROM HIS CHARACTER
   A. Sometimes the sinner makes the attempt to do so.
      1. Conscience is aroused. The Word of God is too plainly against him. Divine providence threatens ominously. Like Felix, he trembles as some Paul preaches.
      2. Partially abandons known sin, i.e., Pharaoh, Nineveh.
      3. Multiplies religious services.
      4. Makes good resolves.

       5. Feels a stir of religious feeling. Tears, emotion.
       6. Self-inflicted punishment, mortification.
  B. Sin cannot be undone.
  C. Sin cannot be hidden (I John 3:20).
  D. Sin cannot be excused.
  E. Sin cannot be expiated by us.
       1. Sacrifice is of no real avail—only a former type.
       2. Penance can atone only for the past.
       3. Future goodness cannot atone for the past.

III. IN THE GOSPEL OF CHRIST WE MAY SEE THE MEANS FOR CLEANSING BOTH THE GUILT OF CHARACTER AND THE STAIN OF INDWELLING SIN
  A. Guilt is shown to be removed by the free forgiveness of God in Christ.
  B. The stain of indwelling sin is shown to be removed by the renewal of our nature.

      ✵   ✵   ✵

30

SIN—LAW—GRACE
Jeremiah 3:1-5

I. SIN IN ITS MOST AWFUL FORM—IDOLATRY
  A. Israelites guilty thereof again and again (vs. 1).
  B. Lost to all sense of shame in regard to it (vss. 2-3).
  C. Had not waited to be tempted and persuaded, but had gone after their sin, greedily, seeking it rather than it them (vs. 2).
  D. Had persisted until the land was polluted by and with their sin (vs. 3).

    E. Had become so hardened that God's corrections failed to produce results save to make them more brazen-faced in their wickedness than before (vs. 3).

    F. Had gone on to this degree of criminality that they dared to mock God with their lip service (vs. 4).

II. LAW IN ITS MOST RIGHTEOUS UTTERANCE (vs. 1; cf. Deut. 34:4)

    A. The law would not hear of the forgiveness and the restoration of those who had sinned in the manner Israel did and had.

    B. Such leniency would open the door wide to the most glaring iniquity.

    C. Sin once committed becomes a fact.

    D. Facts have their necessary, immutable and eternal consequences, which only by a miracle can be set aside.

    E. There is no gospel for the sinner outside the Gospel.

III. GRACE IN ITS MOST MARVELOUS MANIFESTATION

    A. "Yet return again to me, saith the Lord" (vs. 1).

    B. God's gracious purpose of love toward sinful man.

    C. Overcomes the terrible thwarting and hindering of that gracious purpose.

❋　　❋　　❋

31

THE BALM OF GILEAD
Jeremiah 8:22

I. THE DIVINE REMEDY (MEDICINE) FOR THE MORAL MALADIES OF MEN: THE GOSPEL

    A. It is God's actual answer to our human necessities, the sovereign remedy. His love has provided for the sins and sorrows of the world.

   B. It goes to the root of the disease.
   C. It is universal in its application.
   D. It is complete in its efficacy.
   E. It stands alone.
II. THE HINDERANCES TO ITS UNIVERSAL EFFICIENCY
   A. The self-delusion that leads men to think that they
       have no need of cure.
   B. The self-trust by virtue of which men dream that
       they can cure themselves.
   C. The obstinacy of spirit that refuses the divine
       method.
   D. The lethargy and the neglect of those who are sick.

❊   ❊   ❊

32

THE DECEITFULNESS OF THE HEART
Jeremiah 17

  I. EVIDENT IN ITS TENDENCY TO BLIND THE UNDER-
      STANDING TO RELIGIOUS TRUTH
      A. Mind darkened by ignorance.
      B. Mind perverted by error.
 II. EVIDENT IN THE DELUSIVE PROMISES OF PLEASURE
      WHICH IT MAKES, IN THE INDULGENCE OF SINFUL
      DESIRES
III. EVIDENT IN THE FACT THAT IT MAKES EVERYTHING
      APPEAR IN FALSE COLORS
      A. Error assumes the garb of truth.
      B. Piety is made odious.
 IV. EVIDENT IN THE FALSE PRETENSIONS WHICH IT MAKES,
      AND THE DELUSIVE APPEARANCES WHICH IT ASSUMES
      A. Men persuade themselves that they are not

wicked, but their hearts are good.

B. Virtues are magnified; vices are minimized.

C. Persons never converted or renewed are induced to believe that they are saints.

V. EVIDENT IN THE GOOD WHICH WE PROMISE OURSELVES WE WILL DO IN THE FUTURE

VI. EVIDENT IN ITS LEADING US TO JUDGE OURSELVES NOT BY A STRICT INQUEST OF SOUL INTO OUR REAL MOTIVES, BUT BY VIEWING OUR CHARACTERS THROUGH THE MEDIUM OF PUBLIC OPINION OR THROUGH THE FAVORABLE SENTIMENTS OF OUR PARTIAL FRIENDS

VII. IF THE HEART BE SO EVIDENTLY DECEITFUL AND WICKED WE SHOULD BE DEEPLY HUMBLED BEFORE GOD THAT WE HAVE HEARTS SO EVIL

A. We should place no confidence in it.

B. It should be watched with care.

C. We may infer the necessity of a change of heart, and everyone should be led to cry to God for renewing grace.

D. We should come often to the fountain which is opened for sin and for uncleanness.

✻   ✻   ✻

33

THE TRIPLE URGENCY OF THE GOSPEL CALL
Jeremiah 22:29

I. THE LIMITATION IT IMPLIES AS RESPECTS THE PARTIES ADDRESSED

A. To men, not to angels.

B. To earth, not to hell.

II. UNIVERSAL AS THE TEXT IS, IT CARRIES A LIMITATION AS RESPECTS TIME

A. To men in time, not in eternity.

B. To the earth as it is now, not as it shall be hereafter.

C. As respects the individual, God "limiteth a certain day, saying, 'Today, if ye will hear Jesus Christ.'"

D. God has also limited a certain time for our earth as a whole.

III. THE UNIVERSALITY OF THE GOSPEL CALL

A. It is addressed to the entire race and not merely to part of it.

B. "Wide as the reaches of Satan's rage doth His salvation flow."

IV. THE FACT IT PRESUPPOSES AS TO THE CONDITION OF THE WORLD

A. It supposes the world to be in a state of danger, for a threefold call to the earth, so pointed and energetic, implies that no ordinary catastrophe impends over the world.

B. The world is, to a lamentable extent, in a state of insensibility to its danger. It represents the world as asleep: hence the call "O earth." And because that sleep is profound, the call is redoubled. "O earth, earth"; and because the world sleeps on, wrapped in a slumber deep as death, a third time peals the call, each time louder than before.

V. THE GOSPEL CALL MAY WELL BE URGED WITH THREEFOLD EMPHASIS WHEN WE CONSIDER THE QUARTER WHENCE IT COMES

A. It is not of earth but of heaven.

B. It is not the word of man but "the word of the Lord."

VI. THE GOSPEL CALL EMPHASIZED WHEN WE CONSIDER THE PRECIOUS IMPORT OF THE MESSAGE IT PROCLAIMS
A. It is a word of Gospel, or good news, and not of authority merely.
B. It might have been a word of wrath.

* * *

34

DIVINE HEALING
Jeremiah 30:17

I. GOD IS THE GREAT HEALER OF HIS PEOPLE
A. God is not satisfied to leave His people in sin and wretchedness.
B. God designs to restore His people.
C. The restoration of God's people can be effected only through the healing of them. Salvation is not a change of circumstances but a change of the soul itself.
D. It is a great experience to see the source of this healing in God.

II. THE GREATNESS OF HIS PEOPLE'S DISTRESS INCLINES GOD TO HEAL THEM
A. The love of God—love is moved by need rather than by desert.
B. The honor of God—for His Name's sake God saves.
C. The special design of redemption.

* * *

35

THE DIVINE TREATMENT OF SIN
Jeremiah 33:6

I. SIN IS AN AWFUL FACT
II. WHAT IS TO BE DONE WITH IT?
   A. The philosopher extenuates it—imperfection of our nature plus tyranny of the body plus a form of good.
   B. The answer of Despair—inevitable and invincible.
III. CHRIST'S ANSWER TO THIS QUESTION
   A. Does not make light of it or extenuate it.
   B. Does not regard it as invincible.
   C. Promises and gives deliverance from it.
      1. By blotting out the record of the past.
      2. By the present help of His Spirit.
      3. By bright prospects of eternal life in the future.

❊　❊　❊

36

A COUNTRY'S SAFEGUARD
Jeremiah 46:15

I. WHAT ARE NOT A COUNTRY'S SAFEGUARD, THOUGH OFTEN THOUGHT TO BE?
   A. Commerce, i.e., Tyre.
   B. Art, i.e., Greece.
   C. Not strong political organization, i.e., Rome.
   D. Not religious profession, i.e., Jerusalem, Catholic Rome.
II. WHAT IS A COUNTRY'S SAFEGUARD?—RIGHTEOUSNESS

III. What, Therefore, Is True Patriotism?
    A. Not economy
    B. Not education.
    C. Not philanthropy.
    D. Seeking God.

❈   ❈   ❈

37

"WHY WILL YE DIE?"
Ezekiel 18

I. God Earnestly Desires to Save His Children (vss. 23, 32; Matt. 23:37)

II. The Death Of Sinners Is In Their Own Hands
    A. Not written by God.
    B. Not fated by destiny.
    C. Not the result of chance.
    D. Not a consequence of circumstances.

III. We Have Free Will (I Cor. 10:13)

IV. The Death of the Soul Comes Directly from Sin

V. The Reasons Which Lead Sinners to Court Death Should Be Considered

VI. "Why Will Ye Die?"
    A. Because of indifference.
    B. Because of obstinacy.
    C. Because of the love of sin.
    D. Because of unbelief.
    E. Because of the rejection of grace.

VII. The Way of Escape from Death Is Open to All
    A. By casting out sin.
    B. By receiving a new heart. Only God can give that (Ps. 51:10).

    C. Only the Holy Spirit can regenerate (John 3:5).

VIII. WHY WILL YOU DIE WHEN CHRIST HAS DIED FOR YOU?

    A. The divine challenge.

    B. A summons to repentance.

    C. A gracious and powerful appeal.

IX. WHY SHOULD WE DIE?

    A. Death means so sad and so great a sacrifice.

    B. God has done such great things to save us.

    C. The way of life is so free, so open to us all.

❀   ❀   ❀

38

DELIVERANCE FROM DEATH
Ezekiel 33:10-11

I. HUMAN HOPELESSNESS

    A. The penalty of sin.

    B. The burden of sin.

    C. The hopelessness of sin.

II. THE DIVINE DISPOSITION

    A. The negative aspect—no joy.

    B. The positive aspect—that the wicked turn and live.

III. THE JUDGMENT OF GOD UPON SIN (Ezek. 18:4)

IV. REDEMPTION BY THE BLOOD OF THE LAMB

V. "WHY WILL YE DIE?"

    A. Because you are unable to change your own heart (Ezek. 18)?

    B. Because you cannot give up the pleasures of sin?

VI. HOW LONG CAN YOU POSSESS THEM?

    A. You are standing on the brink of eternity.

B. Sinful pleasures are fleeting and transient.
VII. WHAT IS THE DEVIL PAYING YOU FOR YOUR SOUL?
VIII. THE DISASTER OF DELAY
   A. If you delay one moment, you are willing to delay forever.
   B. God asks the question.

❀   ❀   ❀

39

THE VALLEY OF ACHOR
Hosea 2:15

I. VALLEY OF ENTRANCE
   A. Gateway to Canaan.
II. VALLEY OF TROUBLE
   A. Hard lessons yield a rich reward.
   B. Success is the fruit of failure.
III. VALLEY OF RENEWAL
   A. God recalled to Israel the valley of early vows and glad consecration and proposed to make it the valley of renewal.
   B. God invites the wanderer back to the starting point.
   C. God uses the emery paper of rough circumstances to polish His instruments.

❀   ❀   ❀

40

HOPE FOR A BLEEDING CHURCH
Hosea 6:1

I. SMARTING UNDER RECENT CHASTISEMENTS
   A. These sufferings are to be received as from the hand of God.

B. These sufferings are to be regarded as chastisements of God for the sins of the Church.

II. HOPING FOR A SPEEDY REVIVAL
A. Hope rests on the mingled exercise of judgment and mercy characterizing God's dealings with and government of His Church.
B. Hope rests on the regard which God has for the honor of His Name, and for the success of His cause on the earth.
C. Hope rests on the mediatorial prerogatives of the Son of God.
D. Hope rests on the promised power and grace of the Holy Spirit.

III. RESOLVING UPON IMMEDIATE REFORMATION
A. Let us give up the language of complaint and mutual recrimination and substitute for it the voice of prayer.

❀   ❀   ❀

41

THE NEED FOR REVIVAL
Hosea 6:1

I. WE NEED A HOLY GHOST REVIVAL
A. Expose sin.
B. Enthrone Christ.
C. Enlist souls.

II. LET US RETURN UNTO THE LORD
A. In humble penitence.
B. In unfaltering faith.
C. In earnest prayer.
D. In sincere consecration.

❀   ❀   ❀

42

SOWERS OF THE WIND
Hosea 8:7

I. THOSE WHO SOW THE WIND
   A. Sensualists—indulgence of lust—gratification of senses (Jer. 2:13; Eccles. 2:1, 10-11; Rom. 6:21).
   B. Worldlings—hope to obtain solid, lasting benefits in acquisition of ease, affluence, respect.
      1. Riches uncertain (I Tim. 6:17; Prov. 33:5).
      2. Riches multiply cares.
      3. What profit in day of wrath? (Prov. 11:4; Luke 12:19; 16:19; 23:24).
   C. Formalists—"Form of godliness without power."
   D. False professors (Matt. 5:11, 22; Rev. 3:1).

II. WHAT THEY MAY EXPECT TO REAP
   A. A whirlwind is a figure used to represent extraordinary calamities.
   B. Their calamities.
      1. Sudden, despite many warnings (II Pet. 3:4).
      2. Irresistible.
         a. Can withstand fellow creatures (Ezek. 20:49).
         b. Cannot resist God (Prov. 11:21; Ps. 1:4-5; Rev. 6:15-17).
         c. Tremendous.
            (1) Desolation made by whirlwinds (Ps. 11:6; Isa. 5:24).
            (2) Worse than Sodom and Gomorrah.

III. HOW EARNEST WE SHOULD BE IN REDEEMING THE TIME
   A. We are sowing for eternity: every action, thought, word, a seed.
   B. Every moment increases our "treasure of wrath"

or our "weight of glory" (Gal. 6:7-8; Eph. 5:15-16; Isa. 55:2).

IV. HOW BLESSED ARE THEY WHO ARE LIVING TO GOD
  A. There is not a work they do for Him that will not be rewarded (Heb. 6:10; Matt. 10:42).
  B. They sow in tears but will reap in joy.

V. HOW FOOLISH ARE THEY WHO SOW THE WIND
  A. To sow sin is a policy of wretched infatuation; it is like sowing the wind.
  B. The harvest of sin is not only profitless but terrific and destructive; the farther you fall, the faster you go.
  C. It is the whirlwind. All men have sown the wind for all are sinners, but there is "a man" who is able to shelter us from the whirlwind.

❋   ❋   ❋

43

THE GOD OF JUDGMENT AND MERCY
Nahum 1:3-7

I. THE GOD OF JUDGMENT (vs. 3)
  A. God sees.
  B. God notes.
  C. God will recompense.

II. THE GOD OF MERCY (vs. 7)
  A. God sees.
  B. God hears.
  C. God will deliver.

❋   ❋   ❋

44

A PROMISE FOR TODAY
Haggai 2:11-19

I. A DIVINE COMPLAINT (2:11-14)
   A. Am I like the skirt, myself made holy through the birth of Christ but imparting nothing beneficial to anyone else to lead to Christ?
   B. Am I promoting holiness in the world about me?
   C. Is the Lord shining through me?

II. A DIVINE CHASTENING (vs. 15)
   A. Sin has interfered with the blessing.
   B. God is more ready to bless than we are to be blessed (Jer. 3).
   C. God has chastened them that He might bring them to Himself (vs. 17). "Consider . . . upward" (vs.15).

III. A DIVINE CHALLENGE (vss. 18-19)
   A. The disposition to obey has been stirred. Yet because of past sinfulness, indolence, indifference, carelessness, they are fearful.
   B. There is nothing to encourage them as far as the eye can see, but there is the Word of God.
   C. There is no seed yet in the barn; no sign of fruitfulness.
   D. There is nothing visible or tangible to show God's working, but God has spoken, and He challenges their faith.

❊   ❊   ❊

45

"BY MY SPIRIT"
Zechariah 4:6

I. The Spirit the Only Source of Success

II. On What Christ's Cause Does Not Depend
   A. On human patronage or authority.
   B. On human force or the power of arms.
   C. On the carnal policy or the wisdom of men.
   D. On the riches, the learning, the eloquence of its friends.
   E. On moral or social standing.

III. The Cause of Christ Dependent Upon the Spirit of God
   A. The Spirit qualifies the instruments employed (I Cor. 12:8).
   B. The Spirit makes the means effectual (I Cor. 3:7).

IV. The Advantages Arising From This Arrangement
   A. It keeps the Church from despondency (Ps. 46:1-8).
   B. It insures success (Dan. 4:34).
   C. It gives all the glory to God. Who is Paul, or Cephas, or Apollos? (I Cor. 1:26-31).

V. Implications of This Truth
   A. Human instrumentality not excluded.
   B. The necessity of divine influence.
   C. The triumph of the Church is certain. It has already survived the cruelty of Pharaoh, the combination of the Canaanitish kings, the fiery ordeal of a Herod and of a Nero, the malignant purposes of a Julian, the bloodthirsty attacks of French infidelity.

❊   ❊   ❊

46

PRISONERS OF HOPE
Zechariah 9:11-12

I. SELF-RUINED
   A. Gloom.
   B. Chains.
   C. Misery.
II. GOD-PITIED
   A. Called of God.
   B. Roused to a sense of danger.
   C. Encouraged to seek deliverance.
III. CHRIST-RESCUED
   A. A refuge provided.
   B. Stronghold near, open to all, ample for the reception of all who come.
   C. The appeal—"Turn."

✹   ✹   ✹

47

THE HEAVENLY REFINER
Malachi 4:3

I. WHAT MUST BE REFINED
   A. The hard stone of unbelief.
   B. The rough points of self-will.
   C. The prominence of worldly ambition.
   D. The sharp angles of pride.
   E. The ugly faults of temper.
   F. The stubborn marks of hereditary traits.
   G. The dark veins of selfishness.

II. How God Refines Us
  A. With the sieve of sifting.
    1. To remove the chaff of worldliness.
    2. To preserve the corn of consecration (Amos 9:9).
  B. With the rod of chastisement.
    1. To remove from us the folly of wilfulness.
    2. To train us in the ways of righteousness (Heb. 12:5-6).
  C. With the crucible of refining.
    1. To remove the dross of unbelief.
    2. To see the face of His own character in the silver of our lives (Mal. 3:3).
  D. With the knife of pruning.
    1. To cut off the fruitless branches of profession.
    2. To strengthen the fruitful branches of love (John 15:2).
  E. With the fire of trial.
    1. To burn up the evil remnants of old habits formed in sin.
    2. To test the reality of our faith in Christ (I Pet. 1:7).
  F. With the wheel of fashioning.
    1. To save us from the uselessness of an aimless life.
    2. To make us vessels fit for His use (II Tim. 2:21).

❋   ❋   ❋

48

CHRIST'S MAIN MISSION: TO SAVE
Matthew 1:21

I. THE GREAT EVIL FROM WHICH CHRIST SAVES IS SIN
II. THE SALVATION IS FOR CHRIST'S PEOPLE
    A. God the Father with us at Bethlehem.
    B. God the Son for us at Calvary.
    C. God the Holy Spirit in us as at Pentecost.
III. AN OMNIPOTENT SAVIOUR
IV. A WILLING SAVIOUR
V. A LIVING SAVIOUR
VI. A PRESENT SAVIOUR
VII. A PERSONAL SAVIOUR
VIII. A SYMPATHIZING SAVIOUR
    A. By His atonement He saves His people virtually.
    B. By His Spirit, vitally.
    C. By His grace, constantly.
    D. By His power, eternally.
IX. A SUITABLE SAVIOUR
X. AN ALL-SUFFICIENT SAVIOUR

❋   ❋   ❋

49

CROSS BEARING
Matthew 16:24

I. BEARING THE CROSS
    A. Of compassion.
    B. Of intercession.
    C. Of sacrifice.
II. A THREEFOLD TEST OF DISCIPLESHIP
    A. Give up, and take up, and keep up.

1. To give up, we must reach up.
2. To take up, we must look up.
3. To keep up, we must wake up.
   B. Results.
1. An enlarged life.
2. A brighter hope.
3. A sure reward.

❊   ❊   ❊

50

THE SUCCESSFUL CHRISTIAN LIFE
Matthew 17:19-21

I. Abortive Christian Effort—Disappointment
II. The Price of Success
   A. Living closer to Christ in prayer.
   B. Detachment from the world.
III. The Rich Reward of Christlikeness—Increased Influence and Power

❊   ❊   ❊

51

THE GREAT INVITATION
Matthew 22:5

I. The Blessing to Which We Are Invited
   A. All the blessings of grace and glory.
II. Who Are They That Make Light of the Invitation?
   A. They who satisfy themselves with excuses for declining it.
   B. They who reject it outright.
   C. They who delay accepting it for any reason.

III. THE FOLLY AND SINFULNESS OF THEIR CONDUCT
  A. They make light of that which is of the most possible value.
  B. They reject that without which they never could be happy.
  C. They reject that which they are sure to value when it is gone beyond recovery.

❋   ❋   ❋

52

THE RESURRECTION
Matthew 28:1-10

I. THE BANISHMENT OF FEAR
  A. Of sin—guilt, power, doom—Christ died for our sins.
  B. Of death—Christ triumphed over the grave.
  C. Of judgment—Christ is our advocate.
  D. Of eternity (John 14:1-6).
II. THE INSPIRATION OF VISION—"Come and see"
  A. *The Divinity of Christ.*
     Christ is "declared to be the Son of God with power, according to the spirit of holiness, by the resurrection from the dead."
  B. *The Truth of Christianity.*
     "Moreover, brethren, I declare unto you the gospel which I preached unto you, which also ye have received, and wherein ye stand; by which also ye are saved, if ye keep in memory what I preached unto you, unless ye have believed in vain. For I delivered unto you first of all that which I also received, how that Christ died for our sins according to the scriptures; and that he was buried,

and that he rose again the third day according to the scriptures . . ."

C. *The Power of God.*

"And what is the exceeding greatness of his power to usward who believe, according to the working of his mighty power, which he wrought in Christ, when he raised him from the dead, and set him at his own right hand in the heavenly places, far above all principality, and power, and might, and dominion, and every name that is named, not only in this world, but also in that which is to come . . ."

D. *The Hope of Man.*

"But now is Christ risen from the dead, and become the firstfruits of them that slept. For since by man came death, by man came also the resurrection of the dead. For as in Adam all die, even so in Christ shall all be made alive . . . For he must reign, till he hath put all enemies under his feet. The last enemy that shall be destroyed is death."

E. *The Commission of Service*—"Go quickly . . ."

1. First is Christ's part—dying for our sins.
2. Second is God's part—raising Christ from death.
3. Third is our part—evangelize a lost world.

❊   ❊   ❊

53

THE GREAT COMMISSION
Matthew 28:18-20; Mark 16:15

I. ENLISTMENT

A. His program our task for life (Mark 16:15).

1. Universal in its scope—"into all the world."

    2. Individual in its appeal—"to every creature."

    3. Practical in its purpose—"make disciples of all the nations."

    4. Personal in its obligation—"Go ye."

II. ENDUEMENT

  A. His power our equipment for service (Matt. 28:18).

    1. Divine power needed. Natural endowment must be followed by divine enduement (cf. Luke 9:40).

    2. Divine power promised (Acts 1:8).

    3. Divine power manifested: saving, healing, enduring, suffering, sending forth missionaries.

III. ENABLEMENT

  A. His presence our guarantee of triumph (Matt. 28:20).

  B. Guaranteed by His personal presence.

    1. Constant companionship ("I am with you alway").

    2. Sufficiency in trial (Isa. 43:2; II Cor. 12:9).

    3. Rest in the midst of strenuous service (Exod. 33:14).

    4. Comfort in sorrow (John 14:18).

    5. Fullness of joy (Ps. 16:11).

    6. An abundant entrance (II Pet. 1:11).

    7. Glory hereafter (I Chron. 16:27; I Pet. 5:4, 10).

Practical Conclusion: Every Christian is confronted by the inescapable responsibility of carrying the Gospel to others.

—W.O.D. in *The Missionary Worker*

❋   ❋   ❋

54

THE GREAT COMMISSION

Matthew 28:18-20

I. A Great Claim
   A. Material (Eph. 1:21).
   B. Mental (Col. 1:16).
   C. Moral (Phil. 2:9-11).
II. A Great Commission
   A. Astonishing.
   B. Universal.
   C. Compelling.
III. A Great Assurance
   A. Simply true.
   B. Naturally true.
   C. Literally true.
   D. Gloriously true.
   E. A personal, conscious, intelligent presence.
   F. An abiding presence.
   G. A victorious presence. The ultimate victory of the King.

❋ ❋ ❋

55

ADVERTISING CHRIST

Mark 1:40-45

I. The Leper Had a Personal Experience
   A. Smitten with leprosy—sorely afflicted.
   B. Approached Christ with only a partial faith.
   C. Received from Christ a perfect blessing.
II. He Published It Abroad
   A. Advertised the saving power of Christ.

B. Published His saving power extensively by personal service advertising.

III. HE POPULARIZED THE CHRIST
A. Stirred up opposition to Him.
B. Excited interest in Christ.
C. Created a true Church of Christ: "Men assembled in the name of Christ and Christ in the midst."

❅   ❅   ❅

56

SURPRISING FAITH
Luke 7

I. FOUNDATION
A. Unexpected but real, fast.
B. Uninformed but true, full.
C. Inexperienced but firm.

II. FERVENCY
A. Christ—source.
B. Christ—substance.
C. Christ—subject.

III. FORCE
A. For his servant.
B. Unselfish but warm and unpretending but insistent.
C. Working.

❅   ❅   ❅

57

THE TESTING OF FAITH
Luke 8:40-56

I. How?
A. Difficulties throng us—personal, home, business, church, world.

B. Delays touch us.

C. Defeats trouble us.

II. WHY?

A. Try us.

B. Toughen us.

C. Tender us.

III. WHAT TO DO?

A. Only believe.

B. Confess our sins.

C. Consecrate our lives.

D. Concentrate our faith and our efforts.

❀   ❀   ❀

58

THE WRATH OF GOD
John 3:36

I. IT IS SURE TO FALL UPON THE SINNER IN DUE TIME

A. Not a simple possibility.

B. Not a threat to terrify.

C. As sure as God Almighty's throne.

D. Eternal and omnipotent justice has decreed it.

E. Revelation declares it on almost every page.

F. The providence of God illustrates and confirms His Word.

II. IT IS SURE TO FALL UPON THE SINNER IN TERRIBLE POWER AND SEVERITY

A. Here mercy tempers justice.

B. Wrath is restrained and grace works.

C. This is the world of probation, not of final award.

D. The day of reckoning is appointed after death.

III. THIS WRATH IS JUSTLY DESERVED
   A. It might have been turned aside.
   B. Voluntary sin and the persistent refusal of mercy and grace provoke it.

❋   ❋   ❋

59

PREVAILING PRAYER
John 14:12-13

I. THE UNLIMITED PROMISE—"Whatsoever"
   A. His word shall come to pass (Ezek. 12:25).
   B. He is quick to answer (Isa. 6:5, 24).
   C. He is a faithful God (Deut. 7:9).
II. THE UNFAILING PLEA—"In my name"
   A. God hath spoken by His Son (Heb. 1:2).
   B. No salvation in any other (Acts 4:12).
   C. He alone makes intercession (Rom. 8:34).
III. THE UNSEARCHABLE PURPOSE—"That the Father may be glorified"
   A. We are to glorify Him (Ps. 50:15).
   B. He hath made us (Ps. 100:3).
   C. We are not our own (I Cor. 6:19-20).
                     —E. P. in *Moody Monthly*

❋   ❋   ❋

60

PREVAILING PRAYER
Acts 4:31

I. THE CHARACTER OF PREVAILING PRAYER
   A. Unanimous—the Church in a body (Acts 2:1).
   B. United—"with one accord" (Acts 2:1; 4:24; 4:32).

C. Urgent.
  1. The Church exists for the salvation of souls.
  2. All other engagements must be canceled.
  3. All else is secondary.
D. Earnest—"Lifted up their voices to God" (4:24).
E. Scriptural (4:24-28).
F. Believing (4:24-29).
G. Unceasing—"These all continued" (Acts 1:14; 2:42).
H. Pointed (Acts 4:29-30).

II. THE CONSEQUENCES OF PREVAILING PRAYER
A. The place was shaken.
B. They were all filled with the Holy Ghost.
C. They spake the word of God with boldness.

* * *

61

THE HOLY SPIRIT AND HIGHWAY EVANGELISM
Acts 9:6

I. THE HOLY SPIRIT WILL CONVICT US OF THE NEED
A. The commission is clear.
B. The parable is "highways and hedges."
C. No other plan has ever succeeded fully.

II. THE HOLY SPIRIT WILL CONDITION US FOR THE WORK
A. Will vitalize our passion.
B. Will magnetize our persons.
C. Will energize our programs.

III. THE HOLY SPIRIT WILL CONDUCT US TO THE SUBJECTS
A. We know not to whom to go.
B. As in the case of Philip and the eunuch, the Holy
Spirit will lead us.

IV. THE HOLY SPIRIT WILL CONVERT THE SOULS WE SEEK
    A. Here also the Holy Spirit alone can convict of sin.
    B. Here also the Holy Spirit alone can use our message.
    C. Here also the Holy Spirit alone can regenerate.
V. THE HOLY SPIRIT WILL CONSECRATE US, TOO, IF WE GIVE HIM OUR LIVES

� 　✿ 　✿

62

REASONS FOR REPENTANCE
Acts 17:30-31

    I. JUDGMENT
   II. GOD COMMANDS YOU
 III. GOD'S GOODNESS (Rom. 2:4)
 IV. THAT YOUR SINS MAY BE FORGIVEN (Acts 3:19)
   V. IT IS REPENTANCE OR PERISHING (Luke 13:3)
 VI. THE KINGDOM OF HEAVEN IS AT HAND (Matt. 3:2)
VII. JOY IN HEAVEN (Luke 15:7).
VIII. THE FIRST STEP TO CHRIST

✿ 　✿ 　✿

63

THE HEART OF THE GOSPEL
Romans 5:8

I. CONDEMNATION
    A. Sinners by birth.
    B. Sinners by choice.
    C. Sinners by practice.

II. COMMENDATION
  A. God loved us.
  B. God loved us before we loved Him.
  C. God loved us before we wanted to love Him.
  D. God loved us in spite of our sins and short-comings.
  E. God loved us without selfish thoughts or motives.

III. CONSUMMATION
  A. Christ died for us.
  B. Christ died to redeem us from all our sins.
  C. Christ died to reconcile us to God.
  D. Christ died to be buried, to be raised from the dead, to ascend into heaven, to send down the Holy Spirit to regenerate our souls.

God commends that love in the pages of the Bible, in the pleadings of the Holy Spirit, in the invitations of Christians. Will you accept God's love *now*?

✽   ✽   ✽

64

GOD'S CO-WORKERS
I *Corinthians 3:1-15 (9-15)*

I. A STRONG TRUTH—"Foundation"
  A. Salvation (Heb. 9:12-14, 22, 25-28).
  B. Sanctification (I John 1:7; 2:2).
  C. Supply (Rom. 8:32; Phil. 4:19).

II. A SOLEMN TRUST—Gospel (John 20:23)
  A. Salt (Matt. 5:13).
  B. Light (Matt. 5:14).
  C. Witness (Acts 1:8).

III. A SURE TRIUMPH—God's Presence
    A. In trial (Isa. 43:1-6; II Cor. 12:9).
    B. In toil (John 14:16-20; 15:16; 16:7-14).
    C. In glory (II Tim. 4:7-8).

❊ ❊ ❊

65

WELL-DOING
Galatians 6:9

I. A COMMON CONDITION
    A. Some are ill-doing.
    B. Some have become weary.
    C. Some have just begun well-doing.
II. AN EXHORTATION—CAREFUL, CLEAR CONSIDERATION
    A. Weariness may arise.
        1. Physical exhaustion—even Christ grew weary.
        2. An absence of apparent results.
        3. Opposition from those who should help.
        4. Difficulty of the work; unbelief, unconcern.
        5. Prejudice.
        6. Unwillingness.
III. A CONQUERING CONSUMMATION
    A. The reward will be certain—God's promise.
    B. The reward will be timely—"due season."
    C. The reward will be proportionate—II Cor. 9:6.

❊ ❊ ❊

66

ARISE AND AWAKE
Ephesians 5:14

I. A DESCRIPTION
    A. Sleep is inactivity, security (false).

B. Death (impotence, corruption: John 15:5; I Cor. 2:14).

C. Darkness (Rom. 4:18; Mark 7:21-22).

II. A Promise

A. Light of knowledge (Isa. 8:20; Matt. 11:27, 29; Ps. 25:9; Prov. 2:3, 6).

B. Holiness (Jer. 2:25; I Cor. 1:30; Matt. 1:21; Mic. 7:19; Isa. 1:25).

C. Comfort (Isa. 29:19; 61:3; 35:5; 51:11; 57:11; Ps. 84:10; 4:6-7).

D. Glory (Ps. 84:11; Rev. 3:21; Rom. 8:17; Isa. 60:19-20).

III. An Exhortation—"Awake"

A. Love.
   1. Unchangeable (John 13:1).
   2. Self-sacrificing (John 15:13).
   3. Constraining (II Cor. 1:14).

B. Light.
   1. Reveals (Eph. 5:11, 13; Ps. 90:8).
   2. Guides (Ps. 119:105; John 1:4-9; 8:12; 12:46).
   3. Inspires (Ps. 27:1).

C. Life.
   1. Frees (Rom. 8:2).
   2. Sacrificial.
   3. Victorious.

❋   ❋   ❋

67

THE UNCERTAINTIES AND THE CERTAINTIES OF THE NEW YEAR
Philippians 3:12-14

  I. A CONFESSION OF SHORTCOMING
     "Not as though I had already attained, either were already perfect."
 II. A CERTAINTY OF AIM
     "But I follow after, if that I may apprehend that for which also I am apprehended of Christ Jesus."
III. A CURTAINED PAST
     "Forgetting those things which are behind."
 IV. A CONCENTRATION OF EFFORT
     "This one thing I do . . . reaching forth unto those things which are before, I press toward the mark for the prize of the high calling of God in Christ Jesus."

❊   ❊   ❊

68

THE SECOND COMING OF CHRIST
I Thessalonians 4:13-18

  I. RETURN AND REVELATION
     "For the Lord . . ." (vs. 16).
 II. RESURRECTION AND REUNION
     "And the dead . . . air" (vss. 16-17).
III. REWARD OR REJECTION
     "So shall we ever be with the Lord" (vs. 17).

❊   ❊   ❊

69

DEATH TO LIFE
Colossians 2:14

The physical order is a descent from life to death; the spiritual order is an ascent from death to life.

I. THE NATURAL CONDITION OF HUMANITY IS SPIRITUAL DEATH

A. Spiritual insensibility.

B. Moral corruption.

C. Condemnation.

II. THE BELIEVER IS RAISED UNTO A CONDITION OF SPIRITUAL LIFE

A. This new life begins in the consciousness of liberty. "Having forgiven you all trespasses" (vs.13).

B. It implies a freedom from all condemnation.

III. THE TRANSLATION OF THE SOUL FROM DEATH IS A DIVINE WORK

A. God only can raise the dead.

B. God effects it by a blessed union with Christ.

C. It issues in eternal life.

✳ ✳ ✳

70

PRAYER—AN IMPORTANT DUTY
I Timothy 2:1-4

I. FIRST OF ALL

A. First in point of time—"Seek ye first."

B. First in point of importance.

C. First in point of frequency.

II. For All
    A. Our immediate relatives.
    B. Our spiritual relatives: the Church of the living God.
    C. Our nation: "for kings, and for all that are in authority . . ."
    D. For the world at large.

III. That All
    A. "This is good and acceptable in the sight of God our Saviour."
    B. "Who will have all men to be saved."
    C. "And to come unto the knowledge·of the truth" (John 17:3; Phil. 3:10).

—Frederick Rader

❊   ❊   ❊

71

THAT BLESSED HOPE
Titus 2:11-14

I. The Ground of Our Hope of His Coming
    A. His own words (John 14:1-3).
    B. Two men at His ascension (Acts 1:10-11).
    C. He established His supper in memory of His death "till he come" (I Cor. 11:26).
    D. Paul taught it (I Thess. 4:13-18; II Thess. 1:2; Phil. 4:5).
    E. James and Peter taught it (Jas. 5:7-8; I Pet. 5:4; II Pet. 3:1-12).

II. For What Purpose Is He to Come? (Rev. 19:11-16)
    A. To raise the dead saints (Rev. 20:1-6).
    B. To change the living to immortals (I Cor. 15:50-52).

C. To inaugurate His kingdom and destroy His enemies (Isa. 2:1-4; Mark 4:1-5).
D. To perfect His millennial reign (Zech. 14:16-21).

❊ ❊ ❊

72

OUTLINE OF HEBREWS

I. Introduction (1:14)
The theme of the entire epistle is seen here, in germ. God's complete and final revelation is given in the Person (1:1) and work (1:3) of Christ.

II. The Supreme Glory of the Person of Christ as the Son of God (1:5 – 4:13)
   A. His superiority to angels (1:5 – 2:18).
   B. Practical exhortation (3:7 – 4:13).

III. The Supreme Glory of the Priesthood of Christ as Son of God (4:14 – 10:18)
   A. The provision of the Priest (4:14-16).
   B. The qualification of the Priest (5:1-10).
   Practical exhortation (5:11 - 6:20).
   C. The Person of the Priest (7:1-28).
   D. The work of the Priest (8:1 – 10:18).

IV. The Personal Appropriation and Practical Application (10:19 – 13:25)
   A. The new life (10:19-25).
   Practical exhortation (10:26-39).
   B. The first encouragement to progress (11:1-40) —faith.
   C. The second encouragement to progress (12:1-14) —hope.

D. The third encouragement to progress (13:1-17) —love.

E. Personal conclusion (13:18-24).

> He is my altar, I His holy place;
> I am His guest, and He my living food;
> I'm His by penitence; He is mine by grace;
> I'm His by purchase; He is mine by blood;
> He's my supporting elm, and I His vine,
> Thus I my best beloved's am; thus He is mine.

* * *

73

THE SINFULNESS AND DANGER OF NEGLECTING THE GOSPEL

Hebrews 2:3

I. THE GOSPEL SALVATION IS GREAT

A. The deliverance of the soul from the deluge of God's wrath.

B. The author of this salvation—Isa. 9:6; I Tim. 3:16; Isa. 59:16.

C. The means—Rom. 8:3; Isa. 53:3; Heb. 9:22.

D. The salvation itself.

1. Saved from the guilt of our sins (Rom. 8:1; Acts 13:39).
2. Saved from the power of sin (Rom. 6:6, 14).
3. Saved from the contagion of sin (I John 3:9; Ezek. 36:25, 29).
4. Saved from fear (I John 4:18; I Cor. 15:55; Isa. 12:11).
5. Saved from the power of the grave (I Cor. 15:53; Phil. 3:21).
6. Shall be saved from hell and all misery (Rev. 7:17; Ps. 16:11).

II. WHO ARE THEY WHO NEGLECT IT?
   A. Out-and-out sinners.
   B. Self-righteous delayers.
      1. Those who live in any known sin.
      2. Those who trust in their own righteousness (Rom. 10:3).

❊   ❊   ❊

74

FAITH'S FORCE
Hebrews 11:6

I. FAITH'S FOUNDATION
   A. Jesus Christ: Person, passion, power.
   B. Christian testimony: 1,900 miraculous years.
   C. Personal experience: every realm of life.
II. FAITH'S FOOD
   A. Word of God: John 20:31; Rom. 10:17.
   B. Communion with God: prayer heats faith.
   C. Obedience to God.
III. FAITH'S FORCE
   A. Obtains the forgiveness of sins (Eph. 1:7).
   B. Adopts into the family of God (John 1:12).
   C. Receives the fullness of the Spirit (Luke 11:13).
   D. Assures resurrection from the dead (John 11: 25-26).
   E. Guarantees all the freeness of God's grace, the faithfulness of His promises, the fulfilling of His provisions (Matt. 6:33; Rom. 8:32; Phil. 4:13, 19).

❊   ❊   ❊

75

THE BLOOD OF CHRIST
Hebrews 12

I. ITS GODWARD ASPECT
   A. Ground of atonement—a covering—Lev. 17:11.
   B. Ground of redemption—a price—I Peter 1:18-19.
   C. Ground of peace—a purchase—Col. 1:20.
II. ITS MANWARD ASPECT (vs. 24)
   A. Forgiveness—Col. 1:14.
   B. Continuous.
   C. Cleansing—I John 1:7.
   D. Nearness—Eph. 3:13.
   E. Boldness—Heb. 10:19-20.
   F. Holiness—Heb. 13:12.
   G. Service—Heb. 9:14.
   H. Victory—Rev. 12:11.

❊   ❊   ❊

76

HELPS TO PREVAILING PRAYER
James 5:16

I. EARNESTNESS (Jas. 5:16)
II. PERSEVERENCE (Luke 18:4-8)
III. UNION FOR ONE OBJECT (Matt. 18:19)
IV. FASTING (Matt. 17:21)
V. LARGE REQUEST (Ps. 81:10)
VI. SUBMISSION (Matt. 26:39)

❊   ❊   ❊

77

GOD'S CARE FOR US
I Peter 5:7

I. As a Father Cares for His Child—*providingly* (Rom. 8:32)

II. As a Mother Cares for Her Offspring—*affectionately* (Isa. 49:15)

III. As a Gardener Cares for His Garden—*attentively* (Isa: 27:3)

IV. As the Eyelid Cares for the Eye—*instantly* (Deut. 32:10)

V. As a Friend Cares for a Friend—*faithfully* (Prov. 17:17)

VI. As a Keeper Cares for His Charge—*watchfully*

VII. As a Banker Cares for the Treasure Deposited with Him—*secretly* (Gal. 3:3)

❊   ❊   ❊

78

THE DIVINE REMEDY
I John 3:8-9

I. The Saving Son of God

  A. The text has two sides: the dark and the bright; the devilish and the divine; sin and salvation; ruin and remedy.

II. The Disease: Sin

  A. Deep-seated—born in (Ps. 51:5; Isa. 1:5-6).

B. Very old (I John 3:8; Rom. 5:12).

C. Very common—"He that committeth . . . devil."

III. THE REMEDY: THE SON OF GOD

A. Divine (John 3:16).

B. Ready—"Was manifested" (John 19:30; I John 1:7).

C. Almighty—"That he might destroy . . . devil" (Matt. 15:19; Heb. 2:13; II Tim. 2:26).

IV. THE APPLICATION: BORN OF GOD

A. Through Christ (I John 5:1; John 1:12-13).

B. By the Holy Spirit (John 3:5-6).

C. Through faith (John 3:14-15).

❊   ❊   ❊

79

OPEN DOORS INTO THE DEEPER SPIRITUAL LIFE
Revelation 3:8

I. THE DOOR OF PROMISE (Rev. 21:6; John 4:14; Phil. 4:19)

II. THE DOOR OF PRAYER (Heb. 11:6; Jer. 29:13; II Cor. 9:8; Ps. 84:11)

III. THE DOOR OF FAITH (Matt. 9:29; 11:24; Jas. 1:6-7; Josh. 1:3)

IV. THE DOOR OF COMMUNION (John 15:7; Eph. 1:23; Col. 3:16; Ps. 119:11)

V. THE DOOR OF SELF-DENIAL (Luke 18:29-30; Matt. 6:22; I Tim. 4:8)

VI. THE DOOR OF INVITATION (John 7:37; Ps. 23:5; Prov. 18:4)

VII. THE DOOR OF OBEDIENCE (Heb. 11:18; Isa. 1:19; Ps. 111:10; I Pet. 1:22; John 10:10)

❋　　❋　　❋

80

THE EVERLASTING GOSPEL
Revelation 14:7-8

I. THE CONDITION OF THE WORLD UPON THIS EVERLASTING GOSPEL
   A. Men are without the knowledge of God.
   B. Men are without the knowledge of sin, of their sinful state.
   C. Men are without the knowledge of Christ, of acceptance and pardon through the true Mediator.

II. THE CONTENTS OF THE GOSPEL
   A. Its originality.
      1. Not science, philosophy.
      2. Open—undisguised because unashamed.
      3. Successful—has worked miracles.
   B. Its adaptability.
      1. Needed by all nations.
      2. Adapted to all nations.
      3. Offered to all nations.
   C. Its eternality.
      1. An everlasting Gospel because it emanates from an everlasting God.
      2. Based on an everlasting covenant.
      3. Guarantees everlasting life.
      4. Brings everlasting joy.

III. The Claims of the Gospel
    A. Fear God.
        The fear of the Lord is the beginning of all wisdom, the source and guard of every virtue.
    B. Worship God.
        Place the true God on the throne of your heart.
    C. Glory in God and give praise and glory to Him.

✽   ✽   ✽

ILLUSTRATIONS

i

WINNING SOULS
Matthew 4:18-20.

The Methodists had a bishop named Foster. He was a young man, the pastor of a tiny church where former Bishop McDonald's father was chairman of the elders. Foster decided to hold a revival. He was going to do the preaching. He preached two or three days and nothing happened. There were no crowds, no results, no fire, and his heart was broken. He went to see McDonald and asked him what to do. McDonald proposed that the next morning he and Foster go from one end of the town to the other, go to every home, and invite everybody to come to church. The next morning they started out early. Everyone was gracious to them. They came to a house a bit off the road. The older man stopped the preacher and said it was useless to go to that home. A widower and his three daughters lived there, and all were far from God.

He said, "They will insult you, and break your heart. Don't go in there."

Replied Foster, "We promised the Lord we would visit every home. We must not leave them out." So he knocked on the door, and the widower answered. The visitor said, "I am Foster. We are in the revival, and have come to invite you and your children to attend."

The man walked out, closed the door behind him, and said, "Hasn't anyone told you about me? Let me alone. I am not interested at all. I don't want to talk about Christ or the Church. Leave me alone. Let me go to hell if I want to." He turned to walk back in the house, stopped, swallowed, and while the heavy unshed tears came to his eyes, he said, "There's no use worrying about me. But I have a boy who has gone wrong. If you can help him, please do it." He turned, walked into the house, and slammed the door.

Everybody knew the boy. The elder and the pastor came to the livery stable. There in the dirt and refuse, stretched out drunk, was the twenty-seven-year-old son, dirty, slimy, filthy with sin. The men lifted him and carried him to Foster's home. The preacher washed him, provided him with a suit of clothes, and gave him a place at his own table with his wife and daughters. Day and night he kept him there. The boy was converted and got right with God. In a few weeks he left town to get himself a job.

Time went on, and Foster became bishop. He was now a middle-aged man. The Methodists held a conference in Memphis, and Foster attended. One day when he finished speaking a man came to him and said, "Bishop Fostèr, will you come home with me? I asked the arrangements committee and they said it would be all right if it was all right with you." Foster said he would be glad to come. They went together and soon reached the man's residence. It was a beautiful home. They walked in and the man's wife greeted Foster. They sat down to dinner.

Before they began to eat, the man walked to the Bishop put his hand on his shoulder, and said, "Before we ask you to say grace I want to tell you something. This home, my wife and children—all of it belongs to you. You are responsible for it all. This is your home."

Foster, bewildered, said, "I don't even know you. I never met you before in my life."

The man said, "That's all you know, Bishop. I am John Manley, the man you picked up in the livery stable. This is the result of your prayers and testimony."

Each of us can have that same privilege. Say, "Lord, if You can use me, I will pay the price; I will go; I will pray; I will bring people; I will do my best, God helping me, to win them to the Lord Jesus Christ." Oh, the joy, the blessing, the infinite reward of winning souls to Christ!

❊   ❊   ❊

2

THE GREAT PHYSICIAN
Matthew 9:12

Jesus said, "They that be whole need not a physician, but they that are sick . . . I am not come to call the righteous, but sinners to repentance."

There is a marvelous story told concerning an experience in the life of that great saint Lady Huntington. On one of her visits to an English penitentiary she came to the cell of a deeply despondent man. She did not know it, but he happened to be the brother of George Whitefield, the great preacher. Mrs. Huntington could not cheer him, and she asked the cause of his discouragement.

"Lady," he said, "I am in dreadful sin."

"Thank God," she said.

"I am the worst sinner in the world." The man groaned.

"Thank God," she replied once more.

The man looked at her, startled.

"I thought you were a Christian," he said. "How can you mock me by thanking God when I tell you that I am the worst sinner in all the world?"

Lady Huntington opened her Bible to the text we are considering and quietly read, "This is a faithful saying, and worthy of all acceptation, that Christ Jesus came into the world to save sinners; of whom I am chief."

"That is why I am thanking God. Jesus came to save the chief of sinners. There is abundant hope for you," she said.

Right then and there, in that miserable jail cell, the guilty man made his surrender to the Lord Jesus Christ, receiving in exchange for his bitter sins the eternal salvation which was his in Christ.

❋   ❋   ❋

3

"ALL I HAD"
Mark 8:36

Dr. George W. Truett relates this incident in one of his great sermons.

A wealthy young cotton broker was an active member of his church. The man had a wife and a little girl. When the child was about seven she died of diphtheria. Because of sanitary laws, her funeral was held in the cemetery, and numerous friends and relatives gathered about the little grave. Dr. Truett preached one of his inimitable sermons, opening the very gates of heaven to show Christ's warm reception and welcome of that precious soul. When the benediction was pronounced, the undertaker prepared to lower the coffin into the grave.

The father stopped him. Kneeling, he pressed a little silver key into the lock of the coffin and opened it. Some minutes he knelt looking down into the still, white face of his child. Bending, he gently pressed his lips to the cold baby lips. Closing the coffin, locking it, putting the little silver key back into his pocket, he rose to his feet, and linking his arm in Dr. Truett's arm, walked to the car where the grief-stricken mother was waiting. The man, leaning heavily on Dr. Truett's arm, in a voice heavy, weary, grief-stricken, said, "Brother Truett, she was all I had." This statement was not entirely true. He had his wife. He had his business. He had his home. But his peace was buried with that darling of his heart. All else was of no avail.

❊   ❊   ❊

4

CONFESSION OF CHRIST
Matthew 10:32

A certain evangelist tells this story again and again.

He was in his home in Cambridge, England, one afternoon, when there came a knock on the door. He walked to the door, opened it, and in walked a bedraggled, disheveled, dusty tattered gypsy stranger.

He said, "Are you Mr. X, the preacher, the evangelist?"

"Yes," replied the preacher, "I am. What do you want?"

"I have a nineteen-year-old boy," replied the man. "He is out in the meadow in a covered wagon, and he's about to die. The doctor said he could do nothing for him. The boy is not a Christian. I am, but a poor one. Won't you please come and help my boy in?"

Mr. X got his hat and coat and followed the man to

the covered wagon. Climbing in from the back, he ordered the father to draw back the curtains so that the sun could shine upon the outstretched boy. The lad was emaciated, yellow of skin, with the pallor of death upon him. The preacher knelt by the boy's side and said, "Son, I am a preacher."

The boy remained quiet, his eyes closed.

The evangelist continued. "Do you know you are going to die, son?"

The boy nodded his head.

"Son, are you a Christian?"

The boy shook his head.

"Do you want to be a Christian?"

The boy nodded his head several times, his eyes still closed.

"Son, have you been to church much? Have you read the New Testament?"

The lad, keeping his eyes closed, shook his head in response to each question.

"Son, would you be willing to do what God tells you to do to be saved?"

Again the boy nodded. Mr. X took his own little New Testament, turned the pages, and read, "For God so loved the world, that he gave his only begotten Son, that whosoever believeth in him should not perish, but have everlasting life."

"Do you understand it, son?"

The boy shook his head. The preacher read it again and again and again, three times. Before he could say more, the boy opened his eyes and asked, "Mister, can I read it?"

Mr. X said, "Can you read?"

The boy replied, "A little."

Mr. X put his arm under the boy's shoulders and lifted him to a sitting posture.

"Son, you see where it says 'sixteen'? Read right there."
The boy couldn't read well; he had to spell every word as he read slowly, "For—God—so—loved—the—world—that—he—gave—his—only—" and the rest of it.

"Son, do you understand it now?" asked the evangelist.
The boy did not answer but continued to read the verse. He knew it almost by heart, when he shivered and stiffened a little.

This certain evangelist placed him back on the pallet. Spasms of pain crossed the boy's face. He kept on whispering, "For—God—so—loved—the—world—" Mr. X helped him. Again the boy opened his eyes and looked into the face bending over him.

"Mister," he whispered, "does that mean that God loves me?"

"Yes, son, that means that God loves you."

"Mister, does that mean that God gave His Son for me?"

"Yes, son, God gave His Son for you."

The boy was quiet for a minute, then asked, "Mister, does that mean that I can believe in Him?"

"Yes, son, that word 'whosoever' means you and me and your dad and the whole world. It does mean you may believe on Him."

"Mister, nobody ever told me. Are you sure it all means me?"

"With all my heart I know it means you."

The boy looked up at him again, then closed his eyes and whispered, "God—so—loved—the—world—" and all of it.

Quiet moments sped. After a while, with great hot tears coursing down his cheeks from under closed eyelids, the boy whispered, "It means me. It means me. Nobody ever told me. It means me."

The evangelist knelt quietly. The boy whispered, "Nobody ever told me before. It means me. I believe it. It means me. I believe it."

He stiffened, shuddered, and died. The boy was saved, and his soul went to be with Jesus.

�֍ �֍ ✖

5

RESPONSE
Matthew 11:28

Consider Christ's longing for your response. Some years ago a young couple lost their seven-year-old daughter. The wife was disconsolate, brooding, and grieving over the death of her baby. The doctor and the young husband decided it might be wise for the couple to adopt a little child. After considerable time the husband persuaded her to take that step. Finally she consented, but with the understanding that the child would have to resemble their departed darling. They went to an orphanage and discussed the matter with the superintendent. They showed him the picture of their deceased child, and the superintendent brought out ten or twelve little girls between the ages of six and eight, each blonde, curly-haired, blue-eyed, each resembling somewhat the departed one.

The mother selected a little girl and asked the husband and the superintendent to lead the others away. She wanted to be alone with the child whom she had chosen. When the others had gone, she picked up the little orphan and placed her on the piano bench. Gently, tenderly, she talked to the frightened child, told her about her own dear loved one, and asked her if she would like to come home with her and be her little girl.

"If you come to our house, darling," she said, "we are

rich, and you can have everything you want. You will have a nursery, a governess, a pony, many dolls, pretty dresses, toys, as many as you can use."

The girl stood with her little head bowed, her hands hanging at her sides. She said not a word. The woman continued to plead, promise, love, beg. The little girl remained mute. The mother talked about a trip to Europe, about all the playmates she would have, about all the good times that would be hers. The child remained silent. Finally the mother dropped her arms to her sides and stepped back, defeated.

Then the little girl raised her head, her eyes filling with unshed tears as she asked, "If I come and be your little girl, and you give me all these things, what do you want me to do, lady?" The mother sprang forward. Pressing her arms around the little girl, she hugged her close to her heart and sobbed as she said, "Darling, all we want you to do is just to love us—just to love us."

❋ ❋ ❋

6

CHRIST'S CONQUEST

Matthew 22:42

What think ye of Christ's conquests? His achievements? Have you heard the story of the Zulu king who came to London and met Queen Victoria, "The White Mother," as the Africans called her. She carried him through the London streets, thrilling him with the display of her superlative treasures. Toward evening they returned to the throne room of the palace. The giant black stood before her, his hands on his spear. Through interpreters he asked her this question: "White Mother, when I go back to my people I will be afraid to tell them the things I have seen. They will not believe these marvels my eyes have beheld. If anybody had told me of them I also would have said they were impossible. I want to take a message to my country. You are just a woman. Your people are just men, women and children, even as are my people. We have taller, stronger, perhaps even braver men than you have. We have more land. We are a large people. Tell me, what is the secret of your strength, of your power?" Queen Victoria, taking her Bible from the small table beside her throne, rose. Holding the Book before the Zulu chieftain, she spoke. "This Book, O king, this Book contains in its pages the foundation, the secret, the key to the greatness, the wealth, the power of my people."

If only the United States—from the President to the tiniest, dirtiest newsboy—if only all of us would realize that the strength of our nation is Christ and the Bible, what a different story America would have to tell! The Bible is the Book of Victory. The Christ is the Lord of Victory. His mighty achievements have girdled the globe. His magnificent victories have changed the lives of men, the activities of homes, the affairs of nations, the course of a world.

❋   ❋   ❋

7

MOTHER'S CHRIST
Matthew 27:22

Some years ago, in one of the Gospel missions in the city of Philadelphia, during a patrons' service, a well-known lawyer stood to tell how he had become a Christian. He said that when he was about twenty-four he married a beautiful, talented, exceptionally fine Christian girl. He himself was virtually an atheist, at least in practice, without regard for the Lord, the Bible, or the church. He tried in every way to keep his young wife from her going to church and serving God, but, thank God, to no avail. She grew, rather, more devout, more zealous, more spiritual.

After some years there came into their home a baby daughter, a flaxen-haired, blue-eyed gift from the Lord. Mother and child went to Sunday school and church together. They attended prayer meetings, revival services, and many of the other worship service hours conducted by the church. But when the daughter grew to be a young woman, the father took her in charge. She was beautiful, cultured, talented, and the father was inordinately proud of her. He took her to his clubs, on week-end trips, on yacht parties, to dances, to night clubs, and to other places of gaiety and amusement. Gradually the father weaned the girl from the religious ways of the mother, much to that dear woman's sorrow.

On Sunday mornings the father chuckled sinfully as he heard his wife talking to the girl. "Doris, please get up and come to Sunday school and church with Mother this morning."

"Mamma, Daddy brought me in so late last night. I am so tired. Mamma, if you'll forgive me this time, I'll go next Sunday sure."

Next Sunday there would be some other excuse until the daughter scarcely went to church.

The months and years sped, and the girl was twenty. She was engaged to be married to a fine young man. The wedding was set for late fall. About the middle of October, when it is cool in the Pennsylvania Mountains, a group of that girl's young friends accompanied the two lovers on a trip to a mountain lake forty or fifty miles from the city. They chartered a motorboat, got far out into the lake, and had a delightful time. When the shadows of the evening began to fall, they turned for the shore. One of the young men began to rock the boat. He tilted it a little too far, and it turned over, hurling the occupants into the water. They were about a block from shore. They could all swim. Not one of them was so much as bruised, but the water soaked them to their skins. Instead of waiting until their clothes dried off, they jumped into their cars and sped back against the cool, rushing night wind into Philadelphia. The next morning the girl complained of a headache. She stayed in bed. The doctor came and pronounced it a cold. The girl, however, did not improve. The doctor came everyday, and the father called in a specialist, who declared it a case of pneumonia. All that medical science could possibly do— careful nursing, medicines, proper diet— was done for the young woman, but to no avail. On the eleventh day after she had gone to bed, the family physician came out of her room, walked into the lawyer's study, and told him that the girl was dying and that only a miracle could save her life. The doctor asked the father whether he wanted to tell the girl the terrible fact or whether he wanted the doctor to convey the grim message. The man said, "I'll tell her."

He walked into the sickroom, sat heavily in the chair by the side of his daughter's bed, took her hand in his, and began to pat it. Many minutes passed before he could summon enough courage to tell the girl that she was dying, but finally he broke the fearful news to her. The mother began to weep silently. The girl threw herself toward her father.

"Daddy," she sobbed, "I don't want to die! I can't die!

Daddy, I'm not ready to die! Daddy, you've got a lot of money. Isn't there anything you can do to keep me from dying?" She tried to raise herself out of bed, but her father and mother held her down. For some minutes she cried wildly, then calmed somewhat. She turned to her mother.

"Mamma, I guess a person has to die sometime, and this is just my turn. Mamma, do you think it would be bad taste for me to be buried in my wedding dress?"

"No, darling," said her mother, biting her lips to keep from weeping. "I guess it will be all right if you want it that way."

"Mamma, do you think Ralph [that was her fiancé] would mind if I wore our engagement ring in the grave?"

"No, darling, I do not believe he'd mind if he knew you wanted it that way."

The girl and mother kept on talking soberly, softly. The girl's voice grew weak, hoarse with the approach of death. She turned to the father, bowed with his head in his hands.

"Daddy, before I go, there is one question I must ask you. Daddy, please tell me the truth about it."

"Go ahead, darling, I'll do the very best I can to answer you."

"Daddy, you've been saying all this time not to worry too much about religion. You've been saying that if I was a good girl, lived right, and followed the dictates of my conscience, heaven would take care of itself. Mamma has been telling me all these years that if I wanted to be with God when I died, I would have to take Christ as my Saviour. Daddy, now I'm dying. Please tell me—whose way shall I take, yours or Mamma's?"

The man said he threw himself on his child, picked her up in his arms, almost out of bed, pressed her to his heart and told her, "Darling, if you have a moment to spare, for Christ's sake, for your own sake, for Mother's sake, for hardhearted Daddy's sake, take Mother's way."

He said that by the time he lowered his daughter into bed, she was gone. As he testified, he stepped into the aisle in his deep agony, pulled at his grey hair as if he were trying to tear it out, and in a voice husky with emotion cried, "Brethren and sisters, only God knows whether my darling had time enough to take Mother's way."

❊   ❊   ❊

8

GOD'S GIFT
John 3:16

There is an old legend which states that God called the hosts of heaven together for a conference. Seated upon His great throne, He pointed to the earth, and directing the attention of the heavenly denizens to the sins, the transgressions, the iniquities, the disobediences of men, in words torn from His very heart, out of the emotions of His very soul, God spoke:

"In spite of all their shortcomings, I love them. My bowels of mercy and compassion are kindled toward them. They are ungrateful children, disobedient offspring. The tale of their iniquities rises to the very heavens, yet do I love them with an everlasting love and with the cords of loving-kindness would I draw them. But how? The law must be satisfied. Justice must be met. Judgment must find its victim. Who will go and tell them of My love, satisfy My law, pay the penalty for their sins, that I might be just and yet justify those who will hear and heed?"

The heavens grew silent as the city of the dead. The angels bowed their heads in gloomy thought. The saints stood abashed at the unanswered quandary. Suddenly there stepped out from the ranks of the angelic host the mighty archangel, Gabriel. Doffing his sword and his trumpet, he prostrated himself before God.

"Lord of heavens and earth! Thou hast entrusted me with the leadership of all Thy mighty armies. I have done my best and have tried not to fail Thee. Wilt Thou entrust me with this task?"

God smiled and shook His head.

"Nay, Gabriel, thou art the strength of My right hand. There is no task in heaven nor on earth with which I would not entrust thee, but this is beyond any angel. Someone else must do the required work."

Again stillness reigned over the expanse of glory. It was broken by the steps of one of the saints. Tall, stately, bearded, his face shining with an unearthly light, he knelt before God.

"Lord," cried he, "when I was upon the earth Thou didst call me out from among my brethren. Thou didst entrust me with the commandership of Thy redeemed people. With a mighty hand and outstretched arm, in miraculous, wonderous fashion, Thou didst cause me to lead them out of their galling bondage, almost into the wideness of Thy promised land. Let me go back to the earth. Let me tell them the story of Thy love. Let my life satisfy the requirements of the law."

The Lord's face grew sad and somewhat stern.

"Nay, Moses," He swiftly said, "even thou art not good enough. Someone has to pay for the sin thou didst commit, when thou didst slay that Egyptian. Someone has to pay for the sin thou didst commit when thou didst strike the rock instead of speaking to it as I told thee. Nay, Moses, the weight and the burden of thy sins are still heavy upon My heart, are still recorded in the archives of heaven. They, too, can be washed away only by the blood of some mighty victim."

A pall of mourning seemed to settle in the corridors of eternity. A brooding quietness, heavy, oppressive, dulled the hearts of those gathered before God. Suddenly, from the very throne of glory, there came forth a stately figure, outvying the sun in its noonday splendor. It was Jesus. Carefully He removed the crown of glory from His head, stripped the cloak of office from His back, unloosed the shoes of His authority from off His feet, and knelt before Jehovah.

"Father," he pleaded, "Thou didst use me in the creation of these children of Thine. I, too, have loved them and yearned over them. There is but one more thing I can do for them. Let Me go down amongst them. Let Me reveal to them Thy love. Let Me bear their sins in My own body."

God stooped from His throne, lifted His Son, clasped Him to His breast and said, "Go, Thou star of the morning, let that be Thy mission. Fulfill that which from the beginning of eternity we knew would have to come to pass. Go! Let Thy royal blood expiate the sins of a world."

As the lightening flashes from the east to the west, so Jesus left His glory-circled home in heaven and sped down upon the earth. He was born of the Virgin Mary in Bethlehem's manger. He grew to manhood in the silent years of Nazareth, broken only by His visit to His Father's house at His confirmation. In the vigor of His virility He submitted to the baptism of John. For three tremendous years He walked up and down the length and breadth of Palestine, preaching, teaching, healing, working

His miracles. He suffered as no man ever suffered, toiled as no man ever toiled, spoke as no man ever spoke, yet His own received Him not, but cruelly turned their backs upon Him. Gethsemane's agony passed over His head. Pilate's scourge raised the welts upon His defenseless back. The Cross of Calvary bore His torn, bleeding form. Joseph's sepulcher entombed His lifeless body. On the third day God raised Him from the dead. For forty days He walked and talked with His disciples. He ascended up to glory. He is seated at the right hand of the Father. Someday He is coming again to receive His blessed children unto Himself. We are saved by His Person.

❀   ❀   ❀

9

RECEIVED BY CHRIST
John 6:37

In one of D. L. Moody's sermons there is a moving story. A man, steeped in sin and convicted of the evil of his soul, came to the great evangelist seeking the way of salvation. Moody opened his Bible to John 6:37 and pointed to these words: "Him that cometh to me I will in no wise cast out." The man raised the objection, "Brother Moody, I am a drunkard." "It does not say," replied Moody, " 'Him that cometh to Me who is not a drunkard I will in no wise cast out.' " The man said, "Brother Moody, I have abandoned my wife and my children." "That is a dreadful sin, man," replied Moody, "but it does not say, 'Him that cometh to Me who has not abandoned wife and children I will in no wise cast out.' " The man presented a third objection: "Brother Moody, I have stolen; I have been in jail." "Still, brother," softly countered Moody, "it does not say, 'Him that cometh to Me who has never stolen, who has never been in jail, I will in no wise cast out.' It merely says, 'Him that cometh to me I will in no wise cast out.' That covers you without argument or exception." The man was convicted, believed, gave his poor sinful heart to Christ and went on his way rejoicing.

❋ ❋ ❋

10

HEAVEN

John 14:1-6

Some years ago one of the engineers of the Chicago, Milwaukee and St. Paul Railroad, a superb Christian man, built his home by the side of the right of way. He had a six-year-old daughter. Every day the engineer, in passing his home, pulled the cord of the engine's whistle to greet his loved ones. The little daughter got into the habit of climbing on the fence to wave at her daddy as he passed. One day she overbalanced herself and tumbled into the ravine at the foot of the tracks. Her father came home that night to find her in bed with a bruised, scratched body.

"Darling," he said to her, "you must not climb that fence any more. The next time you might hurt yourself badly."

"But, Daddy," replied the child, "I want to see you and wave at you when you go past. How will I do it if I can't climb up on the fence?"

"I'll tell you what I'll do," answered the father; "tomorrow before I leave I'll take a board out of the fence. Tomorrow evening and every other evening when I go past, you can stick your head and shoulders through that hole, and see me, and wave at me."

The man did just as he said. From then on, daily, when the train sped past, the whistle blowing, the child pressed herself through the opening in the fence and waved hand and handkerchief to the much-loved father. The days sped past. The winter came. The little girl contracted a severe cold that rapidly developed into double pneumonia. The man sat night and day by the bed of his darling. The doctors did the best they could, but God wanted that flower in His own garden. The girl grew steadily worse until one day the family physician came out to call the father into the sickroom with the dreadful news that the child was dying. The father and the mother stood at the foot of the bed watching their precious baby. Pale of face, eyes closed, she lay there on her back in her little bed. Minutes went past. After a time she opened her eyes. Noticing the tears of her parents, she whispered in a faint little voice, "Daddy, Mamma, why are you crying?"

The parents, choked with their emotions, were unable to answer. They looked at the good doctor. The doctor turned to the child and, taking her small hand in his, gently told her that her father and mother were weeping because she was leaving them to be with Jesus. Again the child looked up into the face of her father. "Daddy," she said, "you mean I am going to die?" The father dropped to his knees by the side of the bed and pressed his face against the face of his loved child. "Yes, darling," he whispered, "you are leaving Daddy and Mamma to go to be with Jesus." The girl whimpered a little in soft crying. Then she bethought herself of something and began to comfort the mourning ones. "Daddy," she said, "Mamma, don't cry. When I get to heaven, the first thing

I am going to do is tell Jesus about you. I am going to
tell Him what a good daddy and mamma you were and
how you always talked to me about Him. Then I am
going to ask Jesus to take a board out of the wall around
heaven. Every day I shall go to that opening and watch
for you. When I see you coming, I shall wave at you
to show you where I am so that you can come to me."

❋   ❋   ❋

11

THE COMPANIONSHIP OF GOD
John 14:16-18, 23

In my seminary days the matchless Dr. Claggett Skinner
of Virginia addressed us in chapel one day. He told a
story. One Monday, after an unusually trying Lord's Day,
this great preacher saddled his horse and turned his
back on the town for a quiet, God-communing ride in the
woods. He chose a path at random, dropped the reins
on the horse's neck and rode on. Minute after minute
the animal picked its way through the thickets. The
preacher was lost in a brown study. Suddenly the horse
stopped. The preacher looked up. The horse had brought
him into a cleared space. At one end of it was an old
weather-beaten tumbledown shack with a small cleared
garden space beside it. In front of the house, on a
rickety, backless chair, sat an aged Negro woman smoking
a corncob pipe. The preacher got off the horse, dropped
the reins over its head and walked toward the woman.
She did not look up until the shadow of his body fell
on her. She lifted her head, squinted her rheumy old
eyes, looked down again and continued to smoke her pipe.
Dr. Skinner bent over her.

"Mammy, are you here all alone?" he asked.

She made no reply but smoked placidly. Again the preacher bowed to look into her lined face.

"Mammy," he said, speaking more loudly, "are you here alone?"

Once more the old Negress lifted her head. This time she took the corncob pipe from her mouth. Deliberately she moistened her lips. "Jes' me and Jesus," she said softly. Then, after a moment, she repeated, "Jes' me and Jesus, Massa. Jes' me and Jesus."

Dr. Skinner said that the empty glade was peopled with the hosts of heaven as the almost whispered syllables of that black child of God fell on his ears. God was there, and Christ, and the Holy Spirit. The angels were there, messengers of God and grace, attending to the wants of that aged saint. That is right. "Just me and Jesus" abundantly satisfies! "Just me and Jesus" against the world! "Just me and Jesus" against sorrow, suffering, sickness! "Just me and Jesus" against sin and Satan! "Just me and Jesus" against death and the grave! "Just me and Jesus" for all eternity, here and hereafter! "Just me and Jesus!"

❊   ❊   ❊

12

SALVATION
Acts 16:30

Dr. George W. Truett tells the following story again and again. He held a service in his own Junior Departments in his own great church. He gave the invitation. Seventy Juniors came down the aisles for the Lord Jesus Christ. Most of them joined the church. Dr. Truett went about his business. That Thursday he received a tele-

phone call from Baylor Hospital in Dallas. A sick girl
wanted to see him. The little girl, Nellie by name, was
ill with influenza. Her father and mother were with her.
Doctor Truett prayed with and for her. When he started
for the door, the little girl—one of those who had accepted
Christ on the previous Sunday—called him back.

"Will you do me a favor?" she asked.

"Certainly. What is it?"

"Will you go to my department Sunday and ask for me?
If I am not there tell them where I am, and ask them
to pray for me. Tell them Nellie said she wasn't afraid,
because she has trusted Christ."

Sunday Dr. Truett saw that the child was not in Sunday
school. He delivered her message and went on about his
preaching. Saturday another telephone call came. Nellie
was dying. Her parents wanted to see Dr. Truett. He
rushed to the hospital, to find the mother and father standing at the foot of their little girl's bed, weeping. The
child was stretched out on her back. Her eyes were closed,
her face pale with approaching death. Dr. Truett talked
quietly to her parents. After awhile the girl, opening her
eyes, saw her mother and father weeping. Moistening
her dry lips, in a hoarse, small voice, she asked,

"Why are you crying?"

They cried all the harder, naturally.

Dr. Truett answered, "Because you are going to leave
them. You are going to be with Jesus." It took her a bit
of time to understand. In a minute she caught the in-
ference.

"You mean I am going to die?" she asked.

"I'm sorry, but you are. You are leaving Daddy and
Mamma and going to heaven."

She closed her eyes and whimpered softly. Then she thought of something. Her face glowed with smiles. Lifting herself on her elbows in her eagerness, she said, "I'm not afraid. I'm a Christian. I'm going to heaven. Don't cry, Daddy. Don't cry, Mamma. The first thing I am going to tell Jesus is how you both told me about Him, and got me to love Him. I will be waiting for you. Don't cry. Please don't cry."

She continued to comfort her mother and father. The minutes ticked along. Her face grew more pale. She turned to Dr. Truett. He got down on his knees and pressed his ear against her lips. She was whispering.

"Will you go to my department again Sunday? I won't be there, will I?"

"No. You will be in the Sunday school where Jesus is the Superintendent and the angels are the teachers."

"Will you tell them where I am? Tell them I was not afraid to die because I have trusted Christ. Tell them Nellie said for all of them to give their hearts to Jesus, so when they die they will not be afraid either."

That is Nellie's message to you. Oh, let it come into your hearts. Let it fill your minds. Let it thrill your souls. Let it move your wills. You must be saved. God wants to save you. Jesus Christ died to save you. The Holy Spirit invites you to be saved. In this hour, this moment, right now, turn from your sins, put your faith in the Lord Jesus Christ, accept Him and confess Him as your personal Saviour. God for Christ's sake will do the rest. You will then be a child of God, and you will be saved eternally.

✳   ✳   ✳

13

DEBTORS
Romans 1:14

Some years ago while I was in seminary, the good Dr. O. L. Hailey, president of the American Baptist Seminary, Nashville, Tennessee, told the evangelism class the following story.

It seems that when the seminary was but a few months old, the school and he came into financial straits. He traveled to Texas to visit the home of a rich rancher and ask for a contribution or a loan. The rancher was a friend and kinsman. When Dr. Hailey approached him and asked for one thousand dollars, the rancher at once drew out his check book, filled out a check for the sum, signed it, tore it out of his book and started to hand it to the preacher. Before the preacher took it, the rancher asked him what it was for. Dr. Hailey said, "It's for the work of my Negro seminary."

The rancher angrily withdrew the check, tore it into a hundred pieces, scattered it over the floor, jumped up and cried, "What has a Southern gentleman to do with a bunch of Negroes, anyhow? If God wants to save those Negroes, He will do it without you. I wouldn't give you two cents for the whole rotten lot of them!"

In spite of the appeal and protest of the seminary president, the rancher was adamant. Day after day the discussion went on. The cowman absolutely refused to take any interest in the matter. Sunday came. The rancher and Dr. Hailey sat on the front seat of a carriage, while the rancher's wife and father occupied the rear seat, as they drove to church. Dr. Hailey had been praying with all his soul that God might move the heart of this rich man to help in the desperate matter. As they drove along, the seminary president turned to his friend and said, "Jim, slow up. We've got plenty of time. I want to tell you a story."

"Some years ago a party of American immigrants traveled from New York to California. They got lost on the great American desert and ran out of water. The stock began to die, the children to cry, the women to whimper and moan, the men to grumble. The captain of the caravan was concerned about conditions, and early one morning, before sunup, sent scouts in every direction to search for water. One of them set out to the northwest. For hours he rode his horse without sighting water. Toward noon, as he topped a small sand dune, he saw what looked like trees in the distance, a little to the right of his course. Whipping up his horse, he sped toward it. It was an oasis around a spring that gushed out of a small rocky formation, forming a pool about the size of an average house. The man jumped off his horse and carefully watered it. He undressed, plunged into the pool, and soaked up the water with every pore in his skin. He swam to the spring and drank his fill. Coming out of the water, he dried himself, dressed again, filled his water bags and canteens, took another long, thankful pull, gave his horse a drink, got up into the saddle, and turned the animal back toward the party. The sandy expanse stretched out before him. There was no sign of any road. The shifting sand had covered his tracks, but he was plainsman enough to have easily found his way back. The sun was blazing now. He reined in his horse and said to himself, "It's a long way back, and hard. There's nobody in that party who belongs to me. I know my way now. I will just go on and let the rest root for themselves."

The rancher placed his heavy hand clutchingly on Dr.

Hailey's arm, "O. L.," he cried, "you know what I'd do with a man like that?"

"What would you do?"

"Why, I'd tie him to my buggy wheel and take a black-snake whip and cut him to pieces."

Dr. Hailey put his arm around the speaker. "Jim," he said, "What would you do to a man who had the water of life and refused to pass it on to sin-cursed, dying, hell-bound souls?"

He got his check and many, many more liberal ones, so the seminary was saved, and the work went on.

In every direction from us, in every city, in every state are precious souls lost in the desert of sin. We know the oasis. We know the rock that was stricken for our salvation, from whose side, from whose hands, from whose feet and head poured the life-giving flow, even our Rock of Ages. Tell me, shall we stand idly by and drink of the fountain and hesitate to pass it on to others?

❋   ❋   ❋

14

THE LOVE OF CHRIST
Romans 5:8

Two miners in Kentucky were detailed to blast out some rock. They had a fuse and dynamite sticks. When they lit the fuse a bucket was supposed to carry both of them out of the mine. The dynamite was arranged. The fuse was lit. Both got into the bucket. Through some miscalculation only one man had been left at the top. He could not pull both out at once. One of the miners, a Christian, quickly jumped out of the bucket and pulled the rope as a signal. As his partner, who was not a Christian, went up, the one remaining behind cried to him, "I'm a Christian. If something happens to me, I'm all right." The explosion came before the bucket could be lowered again. Fortunately an overhanging ledge of rock saved the Christian's life. It was a heroic act, but the circumstances differed from those involved in Jesus' death. First, for the remaining miner there was a possibility of rescue. Second, it was merely a matter of anticipating a death that was inevitable. Jesus was born to die. He lived in the shadow of the Cross all His days. He voluntarily took upon Himself the form of a man that He might taste death for every man.

❅   ❅   ❅

15

CONFIDENCE
Romans 8:28

An incident happened in my seminary days that will illustrate most fortunately my point. We had a professor there, an old man, a brilliant man, a loyal man, a loving and lovable man, A Christian gentleman. One of his daughters married the son of a great Western layman. One afternoon this professor came to class. He sat down very heavily in his chair by his desk, placed his Bible and textbook before him, bowed his head in his hands, and led us to the throne of grace in the opening prayer of the session. Pronouncing the "Amen," he kept on sitting quietly, head bowed for long minutes. When he did lift his face, his eyes were suffused with unshed tears.

"Young gentlemen, young ladies," said this man of God, "my heart is very heavy this day. I have received some dreadful news. I do not feel quite up to lecturing to you, but I should like to read you a letter. It comes from the father of the man who married my daughter."

The doctor took the letter out of his breast pocket, opened it, and began to read. I do not remember all of it, but a portion of it will remain with me as long as there is a beating heart in my breast and a thinking mind in my head. It read something like this:

"J—, I have some dreadful news to pass on to you. I need your prayer help. You know I had two sons in the Naval Air Corps, both of them lieutenants. The day before yesterday they took off in one ship. Something happened. The ship crashed. They were both killed. The naval authorities wired to my son in Lower California. Without a moment's delay, this son picked up my daughter, and putting her in his own car, started as rapidly as he could to the San Diego Naval Base. As they were hurrying down the highway, a drunken driver swerved to pass a speeding car. He lost control of the wheel and crashed head on into the automobile of my children. Both of them were instantly killed. J—, that is a dreadful double tragedy, aye, a quadruple tragedy, to happen to any man, but I want you to know it is still all right. The eighth chapter of Romans is still in the Bible."

By the time our teacher had finished the letter, we were all weeping.

Anchor your souls in the haven of rest. Jesus said, "If any man will do his will he shall know of the doctrine, whether it be of God or whether I speak of myself." Step out upon the Person of Christ. Close with the promises of God. Anchor your life on the Rock of Ages. The storms may come, the tempests may sweep, the rains may fall, the winds may lash; but he that builds his life on Calvary's Rock shall never perish.

✸   ✸   ✸

16

LIFE FOR LIFE
I Corinthians 6:19

During our Civil War, William Scott, a soldier in the Union army, fell asleep at Key Bridge. He was found asleep, tried by court-martial, and sentenced to die. His mother came to the President, Abraham Lincoln, and pleaded for his release. Finally Abe said, "All right, I will let him go." He took a carriage, drove to the guard house, and walked in. The boy looked up, recognized him, and saluted. The President sat down. The boy stood in front of him.

"William, did you fall asleep? Do you know what might have happened if the enemy had marched over and killed hundreds of our boys? Did you get a fair trial? Do you deserve to die?"

The great, hot tears coursed down the boy's cheeks.

"Yes, Mr. President," he said, "I am guilty and deserve to die."

"William," said the President, "I am going to let you go; but, remember, your life belongs to me."

William went back to his ranks, to his company. The war went on. Came Gettysburg, that fearful battle. William was charging with the Union troops when a Confederate bullet found his body, wounding him mortally. His friend stopped, turned back, raised his head.

William said, "John, there is nothing you can do for me. I will be dead in a minute." He reached down into his blouse and pulled out some trinkets. "I want you to give these to my mother. Tell her how I died." Drawing a deep breath, he said, "Bud, listen! When this war is over they are going to take you soldiers and march you through Washington in the victory march. I want you, if you get a chance, to fall out of the ranks, to go to the White House, look up Abraham Lincoln, and tell him William Scott gave him back his life on the Gettysburg battlefield."

❊   ❊   ❊

17

JESUS FIRST
II Corinthians 5:14-15

Some of you know that when I was converted in 1925 my people turned their faces from me. I have no standing in the family circle. It was a hard, bitter cross of a thought, but there it is. In 1933 when I was pastor in Vickery, Texas, my father came from Chicago to see me, to take me home. He spent eight days with me, and I came closer to hell in agony of heart and soul during those days than I ever expect to be in time or eternity.

I took him off the train. We hugged and kissed each other, got into my car, drove home. On the way he told me about my precious mother, my four brothers, my sister, how much they loved me, how they wanted to see me, and began to ask me to give up my Lord and my work, to come home. I introduced him to my wife. He liked her and said so. I want him to like my wife, and my children who have come since then. It is my prayer that somehow my family may be used of God to melt the hearts of my people and open the way for me to be with them.

During those eight days, by day and by night, I tried every way, I used every method to win my father to Christ, but to no avail. He refused even to look at a New Testament. He turned his back on my Christ. It broke my heart, and I was in deep soul-agony. Night after night he would stretch out his old hands to me and, with tears streaming down his face, in a trembling voice, he would ask me to come home. Night after night I would be obliged to refuse. He would go to his bed, I would go on my knees or face, weeping my heart out.

Came the day of his departure. Together we sat in the Pullman seat. Again he pleaded with me to turn my back on Christ, and the Church, and my humble work; to come home.

He said, "Son, Mamma's getting old, I am getting old, you are our first-born, we have done all we could for you, as sacrificially as we knew how. Won't you come home? We haven't much longer to live. Cheer our old age. I've got some money with me. I'll buy your ticket. Don't get off the train. We'll send for your wife. We've got plenty of money. Come home."

Again I had to say, "I can't Father; it's impossible and out of the question."

He kept on pleading, the tears splashing on his old cheeks, every tear a drop of burning acid on my soul. He kept on begging, pleading, reasoning. After a while someone called, "All aboard." I knew I had to get off. I stood. My father tried to stand with me, but I knew it was of no use, so I pressed him down into the seat. Bending down, I pressed my lips to his: "Daddy," I said, "this is for Mamma. Tell her no matter how it seems, no matter how it looks, no matter how it appears, I love her with all my heart." Then I kissed him and said, "Daddy, this is for you. I love you more than you will ever know. Whether you can ever accept my way or not, whether you can ever agree with me or not, I want you to know that I am just as honest and sincere as I know how to be."

I jumped off the train, got into my car, and started to

drive away, but the tears blinded me. Parking my car near the station, I bowed my head over the steering wheel and poured out my heart to God that He might have mercy on my loved ones.

You turn to me, my beloved, and say, "Preacher, you love your people; why didn't you go? They needed you. They are getting old. They had sacrificed for you. Why didn't you go on home?"

I'll tell you why. All the time my daddy was weeping, all the time I was praying, all the time my heart was breaking, above his head I could see a hill, and on that hill a cross, and on that cross the bleeding, broken body of my Saviour.

Beloved, I may be a Jew, but I am not a dog! If Jesus Christ loved me enough to die for me, I love Him enough, and I want you to love Him enough, so that together we may be ready to live, to give, and to go. God give us the grace to do it.

✳   ✳   ✳

18

PERSEVERANCE
Galatians 6:9

When I was pastor of a certain little church, there was in my membership a great Christian woman in her fifties. She was married and had two children. Her oldest girl was a Christian, who lived with her husband in another town. The twenty-four-year-old son lived at home. The father and son were both unsaved. The father was one of the most wicked, one of the vilest men I have ever known. He never came to church. He abused his wife, misused his children, drank, gambled, committed adultery. He made it hard for his wife to serve the Lord, to come to church, yet that dear woman kept on for Christ, taking all the bitter cursing and brutality of her husband in a meek, humble, patient spirit. The boy came to church almost every Sunday but remained unsaved. Time after time the preacher pleaded with him to give his heart to Christ, but seemingly to no avail.

One night a missionary preached in the church. At the end of his sermon, he turned over the invitation to me. I called the people to their feet and announced an invitation hymn. The chairman of the board of deacons was standing in front of this woman's son. Turning to him, he placed his hand on the boy's hand and urged him to make his decision for Christ. The boy started down the aisle. The people, knowing of the agony in that mother's heart, began to weep. Eight others followed that boy that night to Christ and into the church. The mother was not there that service. The next day I left for a revival in Louisiana to be gone for two weeks. I came back, preached Sunday morning, and at the end of the service stood in the door to shake hands with the people as they filed out. The mother approached. Clasping my hand in both of hers, she pressed it as hard as she could and wept, "O preacher, God surely does answer prayer!" Yes, God does answer prayer. The last man that I baptized as a pastor of a church, before I accepted the position of state evangelist, was the husband of that woman. God had heard her petitions and honored her consecrated, devoted, prayerful, patient, humble life.

❈   ❈   ❈

19

GOD'S BOUNTIES
Philippians 4:19

There was an Irish woman who had a son named Jack.
He drank. One day while under the influence of drink
he was shanghaied aboard a ship going to Australia. After
the ship docked he went into the interior. He discovered
a gold mine and became very rich. Jack loved his mother
and wrote her regularly, every two weeks. He told her
how rich he was, about his wife, about his two children,
his automobiles, his homes. The mother grew old and
tired, but the son could not leave his business to see her.
She finally became too feeble to work. The priest and the
people of the parish decided that she must be sent
to the poorhouse. The priest went to speak to her about
it. They sat over their tea and cakes, talking. The priest
had befriended her for many years and knew she was
a devout Catholic. This mission pained his heart. Finally
he spoke.

"Daughter, I always wanted to ask you what became of
your son. He left home. What happened to him? Do you
ever hear from him?"

"Why, didn't I ever tell you?" she asked.

"No," he replied.

"He went to Australia," the woman related. "He is
very rich now. He has a wife and two children."

The priest asked, "How often do you hear from him?"

"Every two weeks, regularly."

"But doesn't he ever ask about your condition, what
you are doing, how you are getting along, if you need
any help?"

The woman shook her head. "No. He has never asked, and I never mentioned it. I did not want to worry him."

"Hasn't he ever sent you anything?"

"No, except for some small presents on my birthday and on the holidays."

"I can't understand it," said the priest. "He loves you. He has written you every two weeks during all these years. Yet he has never sent you a thing."

The woman replied, "No, except that in every letter there is a little greenish-blue slip of paper."

The Catholic priest was no fool. "What did you do with these slips of paper?" he queried, surmising what they were.

"They looked so pretty. I have pasted them up in my bedroom."

They walked into the room. Pasted neatly from one side of the wall to the other, from the ceiling to the floor, were money orders covering thousands of dollars. That woman did not know what they were, so she plastered the wall with them. She was not nearly so foolish as those Christians who have the promises of God clearly stated in the Word and yet do not have enough faith to claim them. You may live on the mighty bounties of God. You may live on the fat things of Canaan. Your life may overflow with the abundance and superabundance of God's good things. Claim the promises of God. Endorse them by faith. God's bank is always open. It does not close its doors at three p.m., and on Sundays and holidays. Now, this minute, come to God. Acknowledge and accept Jesus Christ as your personal Saviour. Read the promises of God in the Bible. Claim your full part and portion in them by faith. God will do the rest. He is not straitened. He is not bankrupt. There is no inflation with Him. You will not embarrass Him by your frequent and great demands. Claim the fullness of God's bounties in the Name of the Lord Jesus Christ.

❊   ❊   ❊

20

PRAYER — Man's Source of Power

Prayer is one of God's greatest gifts to man.

Prayer is more than a form of words; it has an inner heart. It often seems no more than a heart to heart talk with God; but how many things are made right by such a talk.

The spirit of fellowship transcends all supply of needs and yet needs are supplied.

Prayer brings an answer that is always greater than the thing asked for, it brings the soul in touch with God.

Prayer is a means and not an end. The help we crave and the help we receive is only a small part, — a suspended dream — and God and the things of God are made real.

The great gulf fixed by sin and death is crossed again and again by prayer, over Christ as the bridge.

Prayer may be as mild as a May day or as fierce as an Euroclydon. On the field of prayer, through the power of the precious blood, Satan, self and the world meet their Waterloo.

Real prayer is an inspiration. It carries at its girdle the keys of knowledge and of all mysteries.

Prayer without faith is but husk; with faith it contains the seed corn of a million harvests.

Proper prayer is a mighty engine of war. It can reach around the world; it can touch the highest heaven and shake the lowest hell.

The prayer of faith is mightier than any dynamite, for it has the almightiness of God linked to it.

The prayer of faith shoots straighter than any piece of ordinance, for the Spirit of God sets the range finder.

Prayer is a Jacob's ladder with God's angels ascending and descending taking up the petitions and bringing down the answers.

❃ ❃ ❃

21

WALKING CHRISTIANS

I Thessalonians 1:8

I had a dear friend in Oklahoma by the name of George Murray. He was seventy-odd years old when he died. He came from Georgia. You know, they have a lot of religion in that old state of Georgia. That man was one of the most religious Baptists I have ever known in my life. One night the singer and I had gone to bed in the home where we were staying during the revival. "Uncle George" came walking into our room. We were sleeping in separate beds. He woke us up and said, "Boys, it is too late for me to go anywhere else. I wonder if you would mind doubling up and letting me sleep in one of your beds." The singer said he would be glad to, and he walked over and got into my bed. Uncle George sat down on his bed, took off his shoes, started to undress. Before he moved to get into the bed, he turned to us and said,

"Boys, have you had prayer tonight?"

"Yes, we surely have."

"Would you mind praying with me again?"

"No, not at all," we said.

We got out of bed, and one of us got down on each

side of that old man. He stretched out his great old arms and embraced us. The singer prayed. He prayed. I prayed. We went back to bed about eleven o'clock. That old man began to talk to us about what he had seen and heard. It was a blessing to hear it. When those old-time Christians get started, they surely can warm your heart.

Uncle George said, "Did you ever hear about the walking Christian?"

Fred said, "I have."

I said, "I haven't, Uncle George. I think Fred won't mind your telling me."

"All right, I'll tell you. Out yonder in Georgia where I come from, there was a little village at a crossroad. About a half-mile along the right-hand road there was a little hill. The road went over the hill. Right there at that crossroad lived an old bachelor. He was the last one of his family. He didn't have any more kinfolk left. He was an atheist. He was an absolute infidel. In that village there lived a shoemaker. Every Saturday morning about eleven o'clock that shoemaker would walk from the village store to the crossroad, turn to the right, walk past the infidel's house, top the hill, cross over, disappear. Year after year, every Saturday morning he would go out, and Monday morning he would come back. The infidel watched the man constantly and greeted him once in a while. One time he saw the shoemaker come along, take the right-hand road, start up that hill, and continue out of sight. Monday came, and the shoemaker didn't come back. Tuesday, he didn't come back. Wednesday, he didn't come back. Thursday, he didn't come back. Friday, he didn't come back. Saturday, he didn't come back. The infidel couldn't stand it any longer. He drove to the village and walked into the shoestore. A young woman greeted him.

"Do you have a pair of shoes here?"

He said, "No."

"Do you want to leave a pair of shoes?"

"No. I want to see the man in charge."

"You mean my daddy?"

"I guess he is your daddy. I want to see the man in charge of the store."

"Well, he is not here. He won't be back until next Monday."

"Where is he?"

"You see it is like this. My daddy belongs to a denomination that has no church in this little town. About two miles from the crossroad, on the other side of the hill, there is another little town. There is a church there of our denomination. My daddy goes out there to meeting. He goes out every Sunday and comes back every Monday. He goes to service Saturday night, Sunday morning, Sunday afternoon and Sunday night."

"Where is he now?"

"They are having a revival there, and a great preacher has come there to preach. My daddy is too old to walk there every morning and come back every night, so some kinfolk of ours asked him to come and stay for the two weeks and to go to the meetings. That is where he is."

"Thank you, sister," he said.

He walked out of that door and went home. All that afternoon he studied and mused over the matter. He couldn't understand it. He just couldn't understand it. He had been associating with Christians all his life, but he couldn't understand how any man could have that much religion. He got into his buggy and drove out to the village across the hill. When he got there, he asked the first man he met, "I have heard there is a revival in town. Where is it?"

"You go down past the post office, turn the first block to the right, and go out to the edge of town. There in a meadow you will see a great big brush arbor, and that is where the meeting is."

By that time it was dark. He drove past the post office, turned to the right, and came to the brush arbor where the services were being held. The people sang and prayed. The evangelist preached and gave the invitation. The first man to come down the aisle to the mourners' bench was the infidel. Everybody knew him, knew his reputation, knew his age, knew he was an atheist. They began to weep and praise God. When the service was over, the preacher came up to him and asked, "Brother, we know you have been a hard case. We'd about given you up. Thank God, you are saved. But tell me, what was there about my sermon that moved you?"

The man looked at him and said, "Brother, I don't suppose I could even tell you what you preached about."

The preacher looked as if somebody had dashed cold water in his face and said, "What was there about the singer's song that moved you?"

He said, "Well, as a matter of fact, I have heard better singers than he many times."

"Well, what was there about the service?"

"Listen," he said, "if you will let me alone, I will tell you what it was. Do you see that old man right there, standing by that buggy? He is a shoemaker in my town, and for twenty-three years he has walked Christ. That moved me."

❈   ❈   ❈

22

JOY IN THE LORD
II Timothy 1:12

Many times in my humble ministry have I experienced this flood of joyous feeling and observed it in the experiences of others. Some years ago, in a revival meeting in Ennis, Texas, the pastor, the Gospel singer and I went to the home of a dying Baptist minister to conduct a service. The old man was on the last lap of his journey, with a cancer hastening his end. A group of us met in his room. We sang, prayed, preached the Word. When the service was dismissed, the singer, the pastor and I knelt beside the bed of the sick saint and asked him to bless us. He spread his hands over our heads, and lifting his quavering voice, pronounced a benediction upon our souls and our service. It was a holy hour, and I have never lost the inspiration of it. When we started for the door, shaking his hand, he called us back. Turning to the singer, he said.

"Brother Keegan, can you sing the old hymn, *It Is Well with My Soul?*"

"Yes. Do you want me to sing it?"

The old man nodded. Keegan was moved and stirred to the depths. Walking over to the mantlepiece, leaning against it, he raised his voice and began to sing:

> When peace, like a river, attendeth my way,
> When sorrows like sea billows roll,
> Whatever my lot, Thou hast taught me to say:
> It is well, it is well with my soul.

The room was filled with the golden notes of praise. The ceiling opened. The skies disappeared. The angels dropped their harps to their sides, because there is no

angel in heaven who can sing like a redeemed soul. God
bent down from His throne to catch the glorious notes
soaring from the singer's heart. Keegan went on. He
came to that verse:

> My sin—O the bliss of that glorious thought!—
> My sin, not in part but the whole,
> Is nailed to the Cross, and I bear it no more;
> Praise the Lord, Praise the Lord, O my soul!

The room was filled with the beating wings of the
angels. The old preacher lifted himself to a sitting posture.
His wife tried to press him down, but he pushed her away.
Clapping his hands, in a quavering voice, he joined in the
song. I tell you I never have been so close to heaven
in my life as I was in that sickroom.

❊   ❊   ❊

23

REWARDS
II Timothy 4:7-8

It happened somewhere in India. An old medical preaching missionary was stretched out on what proved soon to
be his deathbed. Two years before that his mission board
had sent out to help him a very young medical preaching
colleague, his wife, and their two-year-old son. The young
man had been forced to take over before he was altogether
ready, but did an excellent job in every way. One late
afternoon the young man came to sit down by the side of
the sick saint to make a report of the day's varied activities. He told about the cases he had treated, about the
souls with whom he had conversed concerning the Lord,
about the worship services, about the agricultural projects,
and about similar matters. When he was through, contrary

to his normal busy custom, he remained seated thoughtfully by the bedside. The old man noticed the young man's preoccupation.

"What is it, son?" he questioned. "There is something on your mind that you have not told me about. What is it?"

"Nothing, Doctor," the young man answered. "It is just a personal matter that I am called on to solve."

"Son," ventured the other, "I am not trying to pry into your affairs, but perhaps I can help you. If you can, please tell me what difficulty you are facing. It may be the two of us can work it out."

For a noticeable period the younger man remained silent. Then he spoke, slowly at first, then with a rush of words.

"Doctor, I have received two letters from England today. One of them is from my home church, a very large affair, with a strong membership as you well know. The other letter comes from our foreign mission secretary. My church wants me to come home and be the pastor if I can see my way clear. The secretary says that if the Lord should lead me to return he expects to retire within a very few years, and it is almost certain that I shall be elected to fill his place. Now, Doctor, what shall I do? You have been here a long while . . ."

"Yes, son, forty-seven years."

"And you haven't got much to show for it."

"No, not very much."

"Your wife and children are gone."

"Yes, my wife and five children. They all died of the same thing, tropical fever. If they had not been in this country they might still be alive."

"You have just a small church building and a very few church members."

"Yes, son, just a one-room stucco structure and fifty-three communicants."

"Well, Doctor, tell me, what shall I do? What would you do in my place? Would you stay here, burying yourself in this jungle, spending a lifetime to have as little to show for it, perhaps to see my wife and child die, or would you go back to England to what looks like the greater opportunity?"

The old man closed his weary eyes. Tears began to trickle down his emaciated cheeks. His lips moved in soundless prayer. After a while, opening his eyes once more, turning to his young colleague, he began:

"Son, one of these days I am going to die. It will probably be very soon. I shall climb the steep ascent to heaven to knock on the pearly gates. The porter angel of God will open them to admit me. After I have registered, he will direct me to report to the Lord Jesus Christ. I shall start down that glorious golden street toward the throne of grace. Before I will have taken more than a dozen steps there will come dancing out from the trees by the side of the street a brown-skinned, starry-eyed Hindu girl. She will grab both my hands in hers, and, dancing up and down in her excitement, will cry out, 'Doctor, I have been waiting for you for a long while. I am so glad you are here.'

"She will notice that I do not recognize her. 'You do not know me, Doctor, do you?' she'll say.

" 'No, darling, I am sorry I do not. There were so many like you in India, I just cannot remember you from the others.'

"She will tell me her name, then say, 'Doctor, you led me to Christ. You baptized me. Will you mind if I take you to Jesus?'

" 'No, child, I'll be only too glad to let you take me in charge.'

"Hand in hand we shall walk down the broadway of heaven. After a while we shall approach the throne of glory. Because He is Jesus, the Master will not wait for me to come all the way to Him, knowing my fright, my heart's condemnation. He will step down from the throne to greet me. Just before I shall have a chance to fall at His feet, the little girl, keeping my hand fast in one of hers, will take hold of the Lord's hand with her own free hand and cry out,

" 'Lord Jesus, this man left his home, his country, his people. He watched his wife and babies die in suffering. He gave up all that he was and had. He was the first one to tell me about You, and I want to be the first one to tell You about him.' "

The old man stopped, almost exhausted, his eyes closed once more. A dead silence pervaded the room. The young man sat there as though he had not heard a word. Minutes passed slowly. The young missionary dropped to his knees by the old man's side, and pressing his face to the face of the departing saint, in a voice choked with heart-thrilling emotion, he sobbed out, "Doctor, I'll stick."

So will I, God helping me. I'll stick by the Christ. I'll stick by the Church. I'll stick by the Great Commission. I'll stick by the Bible. I'll stick by prayer. I'll stick by tears. I'll stick by witnessing. I'll stick by the souls of men. Will you? In Jesus Christ's Name, will you? In the name of perishing multitudes, will you?

❋   ❋   ❋

24

CHARGE THEM TO MY ACCOUNT
Philemon

Some years ago Daniel Curry, a Methodist circuit rider, lost his way on the Nebraska prairies. The night came. It was too late to go much farther. Curry dismounted, unsaddled and hobbled his horse, built a little fire, cooked the little supper he wanted, arranged his saddle blanket and saddle, and prepared to sleep. By the light of the fire he read his Bible, lifted his heart and soul to God in prayer, loosed his clothes, stretched out on the blanket, pillowed his head on the saddle, and slept. He dreamed that he died and that his soul knocked on the pearly gates of glory. The angel opened the gates and asked his name and reason for being there.

"My name is Daniel Curry," answered the preacher. "I have come to claim the mansion in the sky that Jesus promised me long years ago."

The angel leafed the pages of a book on the table by his side. "I am sorry," he said, "but your name is not in this book. There is no place for you in heaven."

"I don't care whether my name is in your book or not," spoke Curry. "I know it is in the Lamb's Book of Life, and I am coming into heaven."

"Do you want to argue it out with God?" asked the angel.

"No," said Curry, "not unless I have to. But if you will not let me in any other way, take me to God."

"Stand still," said the angel. He stepped to Curry's side, put his hand under Curry's armpit, spread his mighty wings, and with a rush, soared into the air bearing Curry with him. On and on flew the angel with the speed of thought. Curry kept his eyes open against the rushing wind. Suddenly he began to see a blazing, brilliant light, as of a thousand suns rolled into one. It blinded him. He closed his eyes to the glare. The angel sped for the very heart of that illumination. Suddenly he stopped and gently lowered himself and Curry to the pavement. The preacher looked down. He was standing on something that resembled crystal glass. He looked up. There on a white throne, high above him, sat one like unto the Ancient of Days, even Jehovah. Curry was stricken with terror. He was face to face with God. His knees gave way, and he prostrated himself on the ground. From the figure on the throne came a voice—stern, clear, solemn: "Who art thou; what seekest thou?"

Curry tried to rise, tried to speak, but fear had entered into his very bones. He could neither move nor utter a word. Again came the voice: "Who art thou? What doest thou here?"

Unnameable dread, horrible fear took possession of Curry's soul. His strength was gone. His mind refused to work. His lips were sealed with the awfulness of the Presence he was facing. Again came the dread speech. "Speak, mortal. Who art thou? What seekest thou?"

Then there came the sound of sandaled feet, the soft murmur of cloth rubbing against cloth. Someone came to his side, bent over him, lifted him to his feet. An arm stole across his shoulders with the hand placing itself on his left breast. He looked over at it and saw a diamond-shaped scar. Daniel Curry knew it was well with his soul. From the majestic figure on the throne came the repeated question: "Who art thou? What doest thou here? What seekest thou?"

The figure at Curry's side spoke, gently as the summer breeze, sweetly as the lullaby of a mother to a sleeping child, tenderly as the cooing of the turtledove in the land. The words flowed up: "Father, this is Daniel Curry. Whatsoever sins he has committed, whatsoever transgressions may blot his record, whatsoever iniquities may stain his past, charge them all to Me. Daniel Curry confessed Me before men, and I am now confessing him before Thee, my Father in heaven."

❋   ❋   ❋

25

NEGLECT
Hebrews 2:3

The Jews have a legend—I have heard my people tell it many times. It seems that a rather wealthy, moral, aristocratic Jew died and faced God at the judgment. The books were opened. His sins were read out, big and little, many and old. When God got ready to pronounce the soul's doom, the man interposed an objection. "Lord," cried he, "I did not know that I had not long to live; I did not know I was going to die. You did not warn me. It is unfair to make me stand before You like this, unprepared, without some sort of warning."

The Lord looked the man full in the face. "Your argument, your excuse, your alibi would be quite good if it were true," He said. "May I point out to you the inconsistency of it? Do you remember when your father died, while you were but still a child?"

"Yes, Lord," the man answered.

"That was My first warning. Now, do you recall when you were twenty years of age and almost died from a siege of sickness that was beyond the wisdom and ability of the doctors?"

"Yes, Lord."

"That was My second warning. Do you remember when you followed your child to its last resting place in the cemetery, and how heartbroken you were over it? You remember how it brought you to the reading of My Word, and, for a little time, to attendance upon My services?"

"Yes, Lord."

"That was My third warning. And that is not all. Again and again, in various and sundry ways, I pressed upon your heart and mind the thought that you were not upon earth forever—that some day you, too, would have to die and face Me."

The message of the story is self-evident. It is my fervent prayer that the Holy Spirit may take these five tremendous words, "Prepare to meet thy God," and etch them on your souls with burning fire. May He give you no peace or rest until you shall have realized your need of forgiveness of your sins and the regeneration of your souls.

✶   ✶   ✶

OUTLINES INDEXED BY TITLE

OUTLINES INDEXED BY TEXT

ILLUSTRATIONS INDEXED BY TITLE

121

ILLUSTRATIONS INDEXED BY TEXT